MEXICO

El Paso

T E X A S

Rio Grande

Rio Bravo del Norte

Ciudad Acuña · Del Rio

Piedras Negras · Eagle Pass

Nuevo Laredo · Laredo

Nuevo Guerrero ·
Ciudad Mier · Roma
Ciudad Miguel Alemán
Reynosa · McAllen
Matamoros · Brownsville

I

C

O

Mazatlán

BOOKS BY OVID DEMARIS

Poso
del
Mundo

OVID DEMARIS

Poso
del
Mundo

Inside the Mexican-American Border,
from Tijuana to Matamoros

LITTLE, BROWN AND COMPANY

BOSTON · TORONTO

LIBRARY OF CONGRESS CATALOG CARD NO. 70–105353

FIRST EDITION

Published simultaneously in Canada
by Little, Brown & Company (Canada) Limited

PRINTED IN THE UNITED STATES OF AMERICA

TO MY MOTHER

Aurore Casavant Desmarais

Contents

Poso
del
Mundo

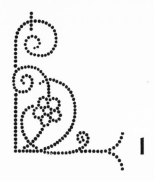

1

Cyprian
Supermarkets

Pssst, pst, señor. *Ey,* americano, *you want a leetle, yes?*
Come here, I tell to you something special. One minuto,
okay? You like girls, eh? I got this booteeful girl, very really
terreefic girl. Her home is Hermosillo and I got her myself
just yesterday. Oh, very young, maybe twelve, but very big
up here, yes? — big teets. Ay, caramba, is she hot stuff, and
clean, real virgeen, and so booteeful, you won't believe it.
So I tell to you what, I make for you the real bargain.
Twenty dollars and I take you there myself for nothing.
Oh, if you want to give me little something for my time,
well, that's okay. But everything first class, just like
United States. We got blondes; you know, long-leg ameri-
cana *blondes. We got everything right here. You want*

nice little show? Two lesbians, real hot show — some-
thing you bet you never see before, believe me. These girls
put on real terreefic show. That I guarantee you per-
sonally myself. No? Okay, how about man and girl? Two
men and girl? Two girls and man? Wait, I got something
you bet you never see before. How about girl and burro?
Girl and two burros, fuck and suck, everything you like,
all positions, real hot show. Homosexual show? Two good-
looking guys, big muscles and strong, you know, muy
hombre; really terreefic show, believe me. How about it?
Ey, wait, I got to tell you about the best dirty movies in
town, in booteeful colors, twenty-six positions, with real
movie stars from Holleewood. No? Ey, what's the matter,
meester? You just want to get drunk, or something? Ey,
come back, I tell you about this great denteest, he fix teets
with real gold. . . .

This exotic proposition, repeated on every street corner
from Tijuana to Matamoros, is the *tema máximo* of the
border between Mexico and the United States, a sixteen-
hundred-mile pleasure strip measurably oriented to gringos with low libidinal thresholds.

Of a long string of ancient, squat, forlorn, sun-dried,
neon-lit oases *al otro lado*, on the other side, perhaps a
dozen qualify (in gringo terminology) as bona fide hell-
holes. To Mexicans in the interior, the border is *poso del
mundo* (idiomatically, the lowest hole of the world). It is
an old opprobrium, gained by some oases back in the days
of longhorn cattle and cowboys along the Rio Grande, or

the Rio Bravo, as the Mexicans call it. Other bordertowns earned their mark later, in the days of revolution and the traffic in guns, gold, and adventurers. It was the Twenties and Prohibition that earned the border its national reputation, and it was the GI of World War II who popularized it on an international scale. Today *norteamericanos* (nór-tay — to rhyme with naughty — ah-may-re-cáh-nos) flock to the other side by the tens of millions, on pilgrimages in quest of everything from jumping beans to saturnalian delights at discount prices.

From Tijuana to Agua Prieta, it is sex that lures the swinger to the border, and from Ciudad Juárez to Matamoros, it is all the fun things that are illegal in Texas. "*Tejanos,*" a Mexican observed, "would rather break our laws than their own." Mexican towns bordering Texas long ago adapted themselves to the volatile steam of puritans in search of sin and cleverly gathered their merchandise in large cyprian supermarkets, fenced off like medieval leper colonies.

Known as a *zona de tolerancia* or *zona roja* to Mexicans, the redlight district is euphemistically a Boys Town to a certain breed of Texans, who, if at times short on loving, are always very long on drinking and fighting. Nowhere is the gringo paid more obsequious deference than in the bordertowns of that big-horizoned country of lean, tough men who come whoring in their work clothes (tight Levi's jammed into stomping boots, flat-topped Stetsons — meticulously pressed in a rodeo roll — pushed back on leather heads), their eyes tense for a wrong move, a no-

nonsense set to their jaws, secure in their reputation as Texans. The Mexican, who is expert at the art of dissimulation, greets them, not like the loud squallers they are, but like the conquering heroes and amigos they are not.

Laredo, like its sister, Nuevo Laredo, *al otro lado*, is Hispanic Western: squat buildings and narrow streets, with the requisite number of fathomless potholes. Ten thousand customers at the Laredo Air Force base have brought prosperity to the area, but it is in Boys Town that the bloom of this bonanza is most in evidence.

A few years ago, civic pressure forced the evacuation of the *zona* from the heart of the commercial district to the outskirts — "Well, *señor*, no town wants to be known as a hellhole, yes?" As a result of this move, the *zona* is the newest and cleanest on the entire border; in fact, two of its brothels, the Marabú and Papagayo, are as posh as anything in Mexico City.

This news could be traumatic to the swingers of Acuña, Piedras Negras, Reynosa, and Matamoros. Of course, there is the other variety here, too — from a leisurely twenty-dollar trick between clean sheets to a five-peso quickie on a *petate* stuffed with cockroaches.

Gene Pugh, agent in charge of U.S. Customs in Laredo, was my guide through the labyrinths of the *zona*. Gene is a Texan, lanky and weathered, and like many gringos in this buffer zone, speaks English with a softly slurred Spanish accent. Some years ago while chasing a narcotics smuggler, he missed a curve, spent six months in traction and many more months learning to walk again.

"I'm not the man I used to be," Gene reminds me as we drive through the *zona's* police gate and into an explosion of neon. "There was a time when I could drink and fight with the best of them." The car groans and staggers in collapsing jerks from crater to crater, like a dinghy adrift in a storm — you feel that at any moment you may have to get out and swim for it.

"Let's start with the best and work our way down," he advises. "It's easier to take after a couple drinks." The best is the Marabú, a barn-sized hall with an elevated dance floor bigger than a basketball court and completely circled by tables. The décor is Mexican Futuristic, which has much in common with Las Vegas Moderne. The girls — the beautiful, *penicillino* clean girls — are strategically deployed to light up the room with the sheer candlepower of their flashing teeth and eyes. But they do not run to greet you. This is a class operation. They just sit and vibrate with sweet promise.

This is familiar territory to Gene. This is where contacts are made and stoolies enlisted in the ever-escalating war on narcotics. The rewards are dizzying — twenty-five percent of the value of the contraband confiscated. A young girl in a micro-mini and pigtails suddenly materializes in Gene's arms. Whores are demonstrative, even in a class operation. She hugs and sighs and holds both his hands tightly in hers. "Oh, baby," she coos before shifting gear into a dragstrip burst of Spanish. The gist is that she possesses valuable intelligence, worth much money, but available dirt cheap. As they haggle over price, in the best *vendedor* tradition, an Amazon in a blond wig turns her candlepower full force in my direction. The first rule of behavior in a Mexican whorehouse, when sightseeing, is never to smile. The second rule is to keep busy, and the best place to do this is at the bar.

The bar's backdrop is Plastic Tropical: a rain forest of artificial ferns and exotic flowers artistically planted in the cracks of rust-colored boulders. To my right, a perspiring customer in shopkeeper blue serge (no *tejanos* in work clothes here — the appeal is too bourgeois) is staring hypnotically at a shimmering expanse of bulging *pecho*. The owner of this generous endowment is a girl with short blond hair and the round face and large eyes of a young Joan Blondell. "Well, what about it," says blue serge, wiping globs of moisture from his upper lip. "How much to take 'em out right here and lay 'em on the old bar?" "C'mon, baby," says the girl, "let's go to bed, I show you everything." "How about it?" "C'mon, baby, let's go to bed." "I'll give you a quarter," he offers, digging into his pocket for the coin. "C'mon, baby, let's go to bed and fuck." He slaps the coin on the bar and she reaches for his leg. "C'mon, we go to bed and do sixty-nine." "Dammit," he cries, pulling her hand away. "Get your mind off the bed for a minute and listen to me." "Okay," she says, "we don't go to bed — we do forty-one, you stand and . . ." "Oh, shit," he says, looking around for sympathy. "Fifty cents and that's top price." She toys with her drink, eyes narrowing and enormous bosom heaving in the throes of concentration. "Feefty cents each," she says. "Fifty cents for both." "One dollar." This exciting dialogue trips along until she pushes back her drink and turns to leave. "Okay," he says. "One dollar it is." She collects the dollar and carefully extracts each breast from its precarious nest. "Feefty cents to kees'm," she says, trying to pull his head down. "Lay 'em on the old bar," he says, brushing her arm from his neck. She stares at him, then shrugs, and leans forward as directed. "Be careful," she warns, as he slowly pours his drink over her breasts. A moment later she is gone.

On our way out, an old friend of Gene's, a civic-leader type in horn-rimmed spectacles and sincere sport shirt, is caught on his way in. "Oh, hi, there, Gene. Well, how — eh — beautiful night . . . , Well, eh, just thought I'd take a look-see . . . Haven't been sightseeing like this in five, six years. Well, eh, see — see you later."

"This should give you an idea of the kind of trade they get here," says Gene. "Businessmen, wealthy ranchers, the best people."

The Marabú occupies center stage in the *zona,* with its own wall encircling its grounds. Neon beckons from all directions, a varicolored blaze visible for miles — an aurora borealis in brush country. We leave the car in the Marabú's parking lot and trudge in ankle-deep sand to a different class of whorehouse, a class easy to find on the border: rickety chairs, battered tables, sawdust on the floor, and cockroaches on the walls. At intervals, terrified rats will make a desperate dash for it — in one place, a rat raced at top speed across the entire length of a cluttered

bartop, sliding and twisting like a broken-field runner —
without once touching a glass or bottle.

This night the only action is from a handful of Mexican
soldiers, teen-age boys in baggy uniforms and drooping
puttees. Cigarettes dangle from liquor-slack mouths and
tequila bottles bulge in hip pockets as they push aging
whores around a wailing jukebox, clumsily copping feels
and spitting a continuous streak in all directions. Pha-
lanxes of whores are propped against the walls. Take your
pick: fat, thin, ugly young, aging beauty, smiling with
teeth, winking without teeth, obscene gestures meant to
be seductive; all desperately eager, all hungry for money
and status, to be desirable, all fading rapidly downhill in a
market that feeds on young flesh. Twenty-one is aging,
twenty-five is old, thirty-five is the end of the line in
cabarets and brothels. The alternative to retirement is to
rent crib space in a *zona* — windowless, doorless, floorless
hovels the length of racing stables, partitioned into areas
barely large enough to accommodate a *petate* or cot, a
chair, a charcoal burner, and a small bureau. A votive
candle burns before the icon of a favored saint, usually the
Virgin of Guadalupe — except when a customer is being
serviced. Day or night, when not at work, they sit in their
curtained doorways, sagging breasts visible under thin
blouses, dresses pulled up, legs apart — rejects from some
impossible horror film — and call obscenely to passersby.

On the road between Mier and Nuevo Guerrero, some
ninety miles south of Nuevo Laredo, there is a *zona* called
Las Tres Marranas (The Three Pigs) which is made up

entirely of crib rejects from other bordertowns. Here the impossible horror film becomes all too possible.

Prostitution is primitive on the border. The Marabú and Papagayo are in a class of their own. At the best *mancebía* in Piedras Negras (it was bursting at the seams with ripsnorting *tejanos*), I watched a floor show while cockroaches literally rained down on the table. After a while, convinced they were racing up my legs, I began stamping my feet to shake them loose and was congratulated by a table of ripsnorters for my enthusiasm.

In Reynosa, where the *zona* is protected by a wall and a moat-like irrigation ditch, I watched a parade meander from out of the brush through the *zona* on its way to Lady of Guadalupe church some five miles away. Made up of impoverished Indians and mestizo peasants, it was a scene out of *Mondo Cane*. On the flatbed of an ancient truck decorated with faded streamers, a little girl, dressed in silk rags and crowned in gold-paper foil, stood very erect, her bony arms and hands folded piously against her thin chest, frozen in the majesty of her being. A band, clad uniformly in rags and playing makeshift instruments, led the procession. Hundreds followed on foot and in oxcarts, many with babies wrapped sausage-tight in *rebozos*. Families of twelve and fifteen in a single oxcart pulled by a lone burro — *padre* and *madre* with *niñita* in front and *niños* crammed in back. Mexican children have to be the friendliest in the world. They are attuned to adults, and respond with heartbreaking warmth. These half-starved children, covered with ringworm and open sores, waved and smiled at the slightest encouragement. They did not appear in the least unhappy.

The children who live in the *zonas* learn to hustle early in life. Few patrons are allowed to leave without an ample supply of Chiclets. A five-year-old will guard your car and vigorously rub the dirt into the paint in hope of a bigger reward. Or he will put a furious shine on your shoes while standing knee-deep in dust. In one *zona*, I watched a group of small boys entertain themselves with a tiny bag of beans, which they kept airborne with the inside heel of their bare foot, passing it from one to the other, in an impressive demonstration of coordination and dexterity — and how they love an appreciative audience. They called the game *chapeté* and the mother of one boy was pulled from a *cantina* to spell the word for me. Although it seems these days that fewer boys are engaged in promoting the virtues of their sisters, there are still too many prematurely shrewd-faced ones tugging at elbows or jumping into cars at traffic signals, incipient salesmen of the glories of cyprian merchandise.

On this day in Reynosa, the whores and patrons came out to watch the parade. It was shortly before noon on a Sunday. Most of the girls still had their hair in curlers. (Never visit a *zona* on Saturday morning — the girls are at the beauty shop.) Later, in what was reputed to be the top house, I found several girls with babies in their arms, and some were breast-feeding. (When I visited the Marabú one morning, I found a group of girls hidden in a far corner busily knitting — for them, the horrors of Las

Tres Marranas did not yet exist.) A group of *tejanos* were taking turns with the same girl, each arrival and departure being greeted by piercing whistles and thunderous stomping. The babies would turn in the direction of the noise, but not one was frightened into crying. (Do Mexican babies ever cry?)

A *zona* is a self-sufficient commercial unit, providing goods and services to its trapped inhabitants at ghetto prices. Each time a resident passes through the police gate, the charge is anywhere from $1.25 to $2.50 for a permit issued for a specified purpose — mostly for shopping, medical visits or a movie. But the *zona* is not the only place where prostitution is practiced. On the Monterrey highway a few miles west of Reynosa, there is a special whorehouse for prominent Mexicans that is closed to *turistas*. And in the towns there are the *bailadoras* (B-girls), who double as prostitutes. Most cabarets and *cantinas* have rooms available for this purpose; if they do not, the girls — after paying a fee — are at liberty to take their customers to cheap hotels. Cabbies and street pimps as well as motel and hotel owners have stables of call girls (and boys). Young girls and widows employed in shops and offices sometimes work the clubs in the early evening hours to supplement their incomes. Even male clerks will occasionally offer their services to both sexes; and prostitutes with border-crossing cards will visit a customer's digs on the American side. All is possible with the gringo's dollars.

Acuña, opposite Del Rio, Texas, has the largest and

toughest *zona* on the Rio Grande. It is made up entirely of cribs and sleazy *cantinas*, and populated by sinister pimps and hard-eyed *tejanos*, who regularly contribute their own brand of squalling to the permanent blast of raucous jukeboxes. The whores are maniacally hostile in their aggressiveness, so that a refusal is interpreted as an insult, which often leads to an unnerving crisis. Beatings, mickeys, and jackrollings are nightly occurrences. Even a drive along its crib-lined street is a perilous journey. I was encircled in a dead-end street by a pack of screaming horrors and only managed an escape by backing up a rutted dirt road at a speed guaranteed to disassemble a car faster than Detroit ever dreamed of putting it together.

Juárez, with a population of nearly a half million, and sixty thousand U.S. soldiers across the river in El Paso, is the queen of the bordertowns. No other place offers as much variety — yet there is nothing here comparable to the Marabú or Papagayo. Although there is no official *zona*, most of the prostitution is concentrated in two areas. The ordinary crib-sexmill operation is in the downtown district on Calle Mariscal (it parallels Avenida Juárez, the main street), and the "deluxe" joints are clustered on sidestreets a dozen or so blocks up Avenida Juárez.

Ask any cabbie (as if you had to) for the best place, and he will instantly shuttle you to Irma's, where his commission is the most generous. If not the best, Irma's is unquestionably the largest specialty house on the border. It offers everything from movies to live shows, and from basic fornication with any of its fifty versatile girls to the

most exotic perversions — a customer's imagination is
only limited by his bankroll.

Prostitution has "always been a sort of wonder" to
Marshall Hail, who has covered the Juárez scene some
thirty-eight years for the El Paso *Times*. "One of the most
amazing things in the redlight districts is the air of innocence on the part of everybody concerned," he says.
"They don't seem to have any qualms; it's just a business
profession to them. They all seem like a bunch of in-
nocents just going about their daily work. Working in
a bakery or something. That's a strong impression I've
gotten over the years. I've no doubt there's tragedy and
bitterness and disappointment and hopelessness, but you
don't see it. When you go over there, they seem to be
enjoying their daily business."

But Hail has also written stories linking Juárez officials
to white slavery rings, and there have been numerous
stories about the *Departamento de Sanidad* — charged
with the monthly health examination of prostitutes —
protecting houses by arresting free-lancers, who are in-
dulging in the only type of prostitution permitted by law,
since organized prostitution is illegal in Mexico.

"You bet there's white slavery," a customs agent told
me. "The Mexican papers carry stories on it all the time.
Much of it comes under the heading of *poquianchismo*.
That's when madams send recruiters into the interior, to
poor villages, and they pretend they're looking for maids
to work on the border. Well, you know, to people in the
interior, the streets of the border are paved with gold. I've

been told this by many girls. If they try to run away, the
Sanidad throws them in jail. The madam then offers to
pay the fine if the girl promises to work it off. The girls
never get out of debt to the madams. They pay exorbi-
tant prices for food, room, protection, pandering, cleaning, laundry; there's no end to it. And most of the girls
have a bunch of kids to support. Many were knocked
up at thirteen or fourteen, maybe twelve, and they've
got kids all over the place. Yes, I'd say these girls are
exploited. They can't come and go as they please. And
the cops and politicians are part of the racket. A lot of the
recruiting is done right in the jail here. After a week in
jail, a girl has been screwed for free more times than she
was in the whorehouse for pay. So what has she got to
lose? It's a tough system to beat. For example we had a
case a while back where we held a Juárez prostitute in the
El Paso jail as a material witness in a narcotics case. So
when she came out we gave her a check for about two
hundred dollars, and she took it to her madam to get it
cashed. Know what she got in exchange? Fourteen dollars.
I raised holy hell with the police, and I know a lot of the
guys, but forget it. Man, it's a way of life."

María, Delfina and Eva González Valenzuela were
wholesalers in white slavery. In the ten years from 1954 to
1964, they provided the market with at least two thousand girls. The sisters' *modus operandi* was to mail "help
wanted" ads to newspapers, asking for maids to work in
upper-class families. Once lured from their homes, the
girls were immediately raped and sent to a training
brothel in the central Mexican town of San Francisco del

Rincón. The best girls were sold at prices ranging from forty to eighty dollars, and the rest were put to work in the sisters' two brothels. Recalcitrant girls were taken to an isolated ranch and methodically tortured until they accepted their fate or died. Girls who became ill on the meager diet of two servings of tortillas and a bowl of beans a day were clubbed to death — one girl was persuaded to finish off her own sister. Another was forced to cremate two dead companions with kerosene. Pregnant girls who failed to get an abortion in time were likewise murdered. In fact, so many were murdered that each brothel had its own cemetery — in one place it was under the bar where the customers did their drinking. The sisters' favorite torture was to place a girl on a narrow board, wrap her tightly in barbed wire and leave her there for days. They called it the *cama real,* the royal bed. When at the ranch, the girls were locked in tiny cells and beaten repeatedly with clubs. "Some died of hunger, some of sickness, and others couldn't take the stick," an employee later told the court. "We sprinkled the bodies with kerosene and set them on fire; then we would call our gravedigger."

The end came when three girls escaped and convinced police in León to check into their story. From the bones found in graveyards at the ranch and brothels, police concluded that from fifty to a hundred girls, including five babies, had died at the hands of the sisters. They were sentenced to forty years in prison, the maximum penalty under Mexican law.

Nogales, Sonora, across the fence from Nogales, Arizona, is the only large town on the New Mexico–Arizona–California borders to have a *zona*. Nestled in a narrow hollow called Canal Street, a short, unpaved path that slants up the slopes of the Pajarito Mountains like a bumpy slide, the *zona* is the only one that is segregated: the farther up the slope, the lower the cost, with the last three or four houses reserved almost exclusively for Negroes.

Then there is Tijuana (good ole T.J. — the Navy's favorite bug-out hole), sixteen miles south of San Diego and "Good heaven, these kids have got to be a million miles from home to fuck these pigs."

Tijuana is the toughest, roughest, gaudiest, filthiest, loudest — the most larcenous, vicious, predacious — the wickedest bordertown of them all. It is all bordertowns wrapped into one smelly reefer and freaked out on its compulsion to "skin the gringo." No bordertown hates the gringo with the intensity of Tijuana, and no bordertown does a better job of separating him from his bankroll.

Here, in gay downtown T-town, the most expensive brothels are barely above the crib standards of Nuevo Laredo. Several are located in the slums along the Tía Juana River bottom (a two-minute walk or a three-dollar cab ride from downtown), in filthy, evil-smelling hovels called motels, operated by *bandido*-type pimps and guarded by hard-eyed bouncers and baggy-pants *policía* — no obsequious deference paid here, *señor*. This is the section where cabbies unload their fares. Another cluster of houses, on the Rosarito Beach road, provides "legiti-mate" floor shows, which usually start after midnight. For the customer who would prefer to remain within the protective glare of neon, prostitution abounds just about everywhere on Avenida Revolución, Tijuana's great gray way. It would be surprising, indeed, to find a nightclub or *cantina* that was not in *the* business.

Stripping, second only to fornicating as Tijuana's great-est art form, contributes immeasurably to the first. Girls strip in relays nearly around the clock, and unless the heat is momentarily on, they waste precious little time in get-ting down to pure buff for their lethargic bumps and grinds. "Oh, yeah," says an *aficionado*. "Man, there's always some half-gassed sailor there at ringside ready and eager to kiss them on the old box. It's a big hit with the crowd." Recently many of the clubs have been featuring go-go dancers who rock with the wild abandon of petulant *vacas* — they go-go best in darkened booths at a $1.80 per three-minute gulps of tea. If the customer succumbs, he can huff and puff in a back room for ten minutes at a dollar a minute. Or if he is apprehensive about certain rampant bacilli, she will do for him — for the same fee — what the half-gassed sailor does to the strippers for free.

"The Americans who come here, many of them feel a little more free than they do in their own country," says Tijuana Mayor Francisco López Gutiérrez. "Well, they are, because you go to a bar in San Diego and it looks like a funeral. Nobody even laughs out loud; it doesn't sound right. Here in our bars, everybody is laughing, making noises — you know the musicians that we have, the *mariachis*. So when they come here they have a few drinks, they listen to the *mariachis*, they can sing, and they think that in the U.S. it wouldn't look right. Just imagine somebody singing in a bar; you wouldn't like that, not in the United States. To us it doesn't matter, for we do it all the time."

Sex on the border — from the Marabú to cribville — is never what it is cracked up to be, in either price or performance, with the former higher and the latter lower. There are endless little extras to be attended to once the initial fee has been paid: money will be demanded by the pimp for the rental of the room, by the cleaning woman for its shoddy condition, by the "nurse" for inspecting your condition, and by the contraceptive vendor for making sure it stays that way. While this is going on, the *señorita* is conspicious by her absence. Once on the scene, though, she will quickly flop on the bed and impatiently await your passionate embraces. But make it quick, *hombre*, there is much work to be done and so little time — *tempus fugit* in *Mañana*land.

Baco looks prosperous. He has a generous waistline and his smooth, round face is smartly decorated with a neat little salt-and-pepper moustache — also dubious proof he is not an Indian. He wears a gringo straw hat and a gringo business suit. Once he was a *chicano*, Mexican-American, but a misadventure with narcotics forced him to jump back over the line, where as a Mexican national he is safe from extradition — Mexican-Americans are entitled to

one free fall. He owns two sections of land on the road to
Tecate, which he is saving to develop for his retirement,
and his children live happily ever after in *los Estados
Unidos*. His place of business is at the corner of Tijuana's Calle Sexto and Avenida Revolución, and his
hours are from two P.M. to five A.M., seven days a week.
With Baco, it is always good business doing pleasure with
you. There is nothing — illegal, that is — that he cannot
promise to supply with alacrity. Whatever the request, he
will reply, "*Sí, señor*. Do not worry. I will have it for you
pronto. You will see that Baco is a man of his word."
Well, you think maybe you could get me a little junk?
"*Sí, señor*. Do not worry. I will be back in twenty minutes
with all you want of the very finest quality." A nine-year-
old virgin? "*Sí, señor*. Do not worry. My cousin has been
saving his beautiful daughter these many years for an
americano such as you." How about a hot movie in technicolor? "*Sí, señor*. Do not worry. I will get for you the
very finest movie in the most beautiful colors." But, Baco,
this is black and white? "*Sí, señor*. Do not worry. Black
and white, that is color, yes?" I would like to know all the
names of the big dope traffickers for the FBI. "*Sí, señor*.
Do not worry. I will get for you many fine names."
Really? "*Sí, señor*. Do not worry. Baco is a man of his
word, *muy honrado*." Whatever Baco may be, noblesse
oblige is not part of it — Baco is a Tijuana cabbie.

However, few cabbies are as respectable as Baco in ap-
pearance. Most look like fugitives from a bad Western.
And none are interested in transporting you anywhere but

to a whorehouse — even at ten o'clock in the morning. A tourist must keep two rules in mind: First, never enter a cab without first having ascertained the fee. By federal law, the flat rate from the border to downtown Tijuana is set at twenty-five cents; however, the fee agreed upon will never be less than a dollar, and, if you neglect to bargain, it may well be three to five dollars. And, second, after you get into the cab, whatever the charge, do not fight over it. Pay it and chalk it up to experience. The cabbies have the strongest union in Tijuana. They never go to jail — you do. A few years ago, the cabdrivers' union in Juárez closed the border by blockading the port.

"Yes, we have big problem with cabdrivers," says Mayor López. "Yes, we do. Just a terrible problem, but you see they are not as bad as they used to be, but they want to be the owners of the city. They do whatever they like here. They want no controls. It is very difficult for us. We are trying to get the Tourist Department to put meters in the cabs, but it is not our jurisdiction, you see. It belongs to the federal government."

No bordertown is a place for a family outing at night. After a certain hour, the pimps get restless and begin propositioning everything that moves into their line of vision. Sidestreets, most of which would make a haven of Central Park, are to be avoided, whatever the sacrifice. Better still, amigo, the easiest sacrifice of all would be to stay home.

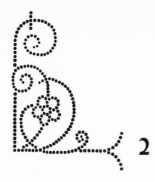

2

Al Otro Lado

History on the border is as thick as dust. Centuries before the white man discovered the New World, tribes of nomads, known as Coahuiltecans, wandered along the banks of the Rio Grande. They are extinct now, and gone are most of the Comanche who raided the small villages and ranches along the river. The last century was a time of bloody upheaval: the Texas Revolution; the Miers Expedition of some three hundred ripsnorting *tejanos* looking for a rumble *al otro lado* and finding instead death and imprisonment; the Mexican War (Yankee Invasion to Mexicans) and Zack Taylor's cannon balls over the Rio Grande; the American Civil War and the Confederate shipping of cotton to England via Matamoros to bypass the Union blockade.

Ey, hombre, this is where the West was born. Texas
Rangers and longhorn cattle, gringo renegades and som-
breroed *bandidos,* cattle thieves, and fast guns; and general mayhem on both sides of the river — sometimes
smack-dab in the middle of it.

Cheno Cortina was the Red Robber of the Rio Grande,
but he claimed he was only retrieving *el ganado de Nanita*
— Grandma's cattle. It was Cheno who crossed the river
to burn Roma, and years later Marlon Brando rode
through Roma's streets as Emiliano Zapata, the revolutionist whose handsome head ended up on a spike in
front of his home. Another revolutionist, Doroteo
"Pancho Villa" Arango, crossed the Rio Grande to kill
New Mexicans because President Wilson had cut off his
supply of lend-lease arms. General John J. "Black Jack"
Pershing spent several exhausting months chasing up and
down the mountains of Chihuahua in a vain search for
the elusive Villa — long before any of us knew he looked
like Wallace Beery, *et al.*

Those were the days when much of the best grazing
land in the northern states of Mexico was owned by
gringo cattle barons, a situation that was to change radi-
cally following the Mexican Revolution. Great fortunes
were made on both sides during the Revolution, and
lasting friendships were cemented between rebel leaders
and smugglers of the tools of war.

Wirt G. Bowman first came to Nogales, Arizona, in
1897 to work for the railroad. He made his first fortune
buying cattle when the Revolution spread to Sonora and

ranchers desperately drove their herds to the border before they were seized by the Army or rebels. It was a buyer's market; and with the profits, Bowman purchased arms and ammunition, which placed him not only in a seller's market but very close to the elbow of such Revolutionary heroes as Alvaro Obregón, Plutarco Elías Calles and Abelardo Rodríguez, all of Sonora and all headed for the presidency. Bowman found another seller's market during Prohibition. Later he took his bankroll to the gambling camps of Tijuana and, along with Rodríguez, was one of the impresarios at Agua Caliente (see Chapter 7). When gambling was outlawed in 1935, Bowman returned to Nogales and was elected mayor. He bought the First National Bank of Nogales and for eight years was Democratic National Committeeman for Arizona. His career came full circle when he was appointed Collector of Customs for Arizona, serving from 1943 until his death in 1946.

Not all Mexican soldiers were involved in the Revolution. General Esteban Cantú first came to the Territory of Baja California del Norte in 1911 to drive out the filibusters. In the next nine years, he not only kept the Revolution out of his domain but its new paper money as well. The only medium of exchange he recognized was gold. All efforts by Villa or Venustiano Carranza to enlist Cantú's aid or gold were rebuffed. Compared to the rest of Mexico, Baja was a happy valley during the Revolution. Cantú's problems came after the Revolution. In 1920 the provisional government offered paper for his gold, and he responded by shipping it to banks in San Diego. He was declared in revolt, and General Abelardo Rodríguez and five thousand fierce Yaqui Indians were dispatched to straighten him out. Cantú retaliated by recruiting three thousand Yaquis — this was how Revolutionary generals terrified one another. San Diegans urged Cantú to secede and make an independent republic. Arms and ammunition, along with unemployed doughboys, streamed over the border to his defense. But Cantú capitulated without firing a shot. He yielded to replacement and was demoted in rank to colonel. From there he went to Los Angeles to lose his money to sharp operators.

The earthquake that killed the Barbary Coast dispossessed a great many hustlers, who swept south, vultures on the wing for fresher carrion, all the way to Tijuana, then a town of less than a thousand people, but already called by many "the worst hellhole on earth." But to the hustlers it was familiar country — for many years a San Franciscan walking its wide dusty main street would recognize a proprietor or bartender in all the bigger dives.

What was it like in Tijuana on the eve of Prohibition? A New York *Times* story described it this way: "You forget everything in amazement at finding yourself in what strikes you at first as a recrudescence of a Bret Harte mining camp or a Wild West main street scene in the movies, with a dash of Coney Island thrown in. . . . On either side is a succession of saloons, dance halls, moving picture barns and gambling dens. . . . The air reeks of dust, warm humanity, toilet perfume, stale tobacco. . . . The welkin rings and vibrates with the laughter and chatter of abnormal good spirits, the noise of an occasional fracas, the whirl of the roulette wheel . . . the tap-tap-tap of hammers where new joy palaces are being shot up overnight to accommodate the business of the prohibition boomtown, and, above all, the continuous jangle of jazz."

One of the early joy palaces in Tijuana belonged to Wirt G. Bowman from Nogales. It was the Foreign Club, which occupied nearly a full downtown block. (The building is still there.) One old timer remembers it well: "It was so beautiful, it made you feel like drinking and gambling even if you hated it. They had all the best people, and it was nothing like Las Vegas today, with the hoods all over the place. This was class. Let me give you an example of what I mean. There was this little jockey, Little Eddie, who hurt his neck in a fall and developed a muscle spasm, something like a tick: his neck would twitch and his head would snap and his eyes would kind of roll around — quite interesting to watch, really. Well, he was very popular and like most jockeys, a really elegant dresser. His job was to collect silver dollars from the tables for the cashier. But Little Eddie had a little larceny, you see. He had a special belt made to hold silver dollars and he would slip in a few on each trip to the cashier. One day the belt broke and there went the silver dollars, clanking all over the marble floor, and there was Little Eddie, just looking kind of wild, with his neck twitching and his head snapping and his eyes rolling around like they were about to pop out. Well, in Vegas they would have taken care of his twitch for him. But here they only fired him, and later we heard he was suing the belt company; it was supposed to be guaranteed."

The more things change the more . . . :

"The booze flowed across the border in those days like marijuana does today," recalls Aron Quick, a retired U.S. Customs agent. "A lot of it came through the ports in automobiles. They had secret compartments in the door panels, tanks under the rear seat and along the drive shaft. A regular passenger car could carry about a hundred and ten gallons. The trick was to rock the car and listen for a splashing sound. And they got it out in trucks and air-planes and small boats from a thousand spots. A lot of prominent families on both sides made their fortunes in bootleg booze. The Prohibition agents were just no damn good."

The strong breath of Prohibition blew life into many bordertowns. Dry *americanos* descended upon the bars in droves and the cash registers rang with joy from noon to noon. *Señoritas* danced and *mariachis* sang and cocks fought and bulls died and gringos guzzled. *Ay, caramba:* — what about *papacita* and *mamacita* and *niños* and those not so *niño* anymore. *Hijo de la chingada,* behind the wall, *rápido,* topped with broken glass, and *alto,* amigo.

Here on the border, the halcyon days of ribaldry need never die. They are reclaimable on notice. Here in a hard land, where life is too real and earnest for its citizens, foreigners find an escape into a weird house of cracked mirrors, to indulge the darkest reflection of their split-image.

What else is there for the *turista* on the other side? Well, of course, there is always souvenir hunting, another great American sport. ("Come and get me," cried the Nip soldier from his World War II cave, "you souvenir hunting sonofabitch.") All sorts of curios are available, even some made in Hoboken. There is turquoise-and-silver jewelry, sombreros, serapes, guitars, bongo drums, leather goods in every shape and form, pornographic towels, sexy ashtrays, red-hot Jalapeña peppers, fried bananas, charcoal-roasted corn on the cob, fiery *tacos* (with a pretty hot bacteria count), switchblades, jumping beans, garish iridescent velour paintings, Chiclets, abortions, balloons, *piñatas*, earthen casseroles, baskets, cheap quickie marriages and equally quick but less cheap divorces, wrought-iron monstrosities, false teeth, second-rate "showtime" bullfights, third-rate horse races in Tijuana and Juárez, and *rápido jai alai* in Tijuana when the union is not on strike. In the free ports (tax-free areas on certain imports) there are English woolens, German cuckoo clocks and Swiss watches which don't work too well once on American soil, and French perfumes. I bought a thirty-dollar bottle of Joy in Tijuana and a twenty-dollar one in Nogales. Both were unsealed and ninety percent water. Or you may mount a zebra-striped burro to have your picture taken in a serape and sombrero — an invaluable conversation piece.

The bulls are so inferior in Tijuana that they often run through all the spares before they can find one that will fight. Besides their obviously shaved horns, the bulls are either too old or too young, too weak or too small, or too blind or too cowardly. Most are rejects from Guadalajara, where bullfighting follows a more classical approach. Bellowing gringos with phony wineskins a la Hemingway do not inspire *toreros* in their moment of truth. The result is showtime.

"Most of the bullfighters I met were terribly crude," says Nancy, an attractive blonde from San Diego who wished to remain anonymous. "They behaved like guys on the street; you know, a street-gang type of mentality. I was with a bullfighter one night who got mad at the host who had thrown a party in his honor and went out in the garage and let the air out of all the tires on his car. No class. And they're always telling you about how dangerous it is in the ring, and their fear of being gored. It's such a preoccupation with them. It's on their mind all the time. Most are on pills. The pills are always there, and after a while you take them for granted. I was in Mexico City, following Raul García on his tour three years ago, and when he left he gave me a present — it was marijuana. They use it so freely that it seems very acceptable to them."

As chief of the U.S. Consulate's protection and welfare section in Tijuana, Jack Bartelt is confronted by ten thousand Americans in trouble each year. "I get calls every day," he says, "from American women who want me to recommend a good doctor. When I ask them what kind, they usually hem and haw and say general practitioner. I say, 'Forget it.' And they say, very innocently, 'What do you mean?' I say, 'Lady, keep the hell out of here. The only guys performing abortions around here are electricians and plumbers.' But, of course, many doctors *are* performing abortions, and most women who come here have already made arrangements through their own doctors. Some doctors actually encourage their patients to come to Tijuana, particularly young unmarried girls. My opinion of these doctors is unprintable."

Tijuana and Enseñada, combined, form the abortion capital of the Western Hemisphere. Recently the California Bureau of Criminal Identification and Investigation conducted a telephone survey of seventy-seven doctors selected at random from the Tijuana directory. Twenty-seven agreed on the first call to perform an abortion, five suggested further consultation in their office, and forty-five demurred; but at least fifty percent in this latter group appeared open to further persuasion.

For years the Paris Clinic, which recently went out of action, was the biggest and classiest abortion mill in Tijuana. It provided a whole coterie of movie stars with well-publicized "miscarriages." The director, a leading surgeon, donated his morning hours to the local hospital; in the afternoon, he tended to his private practice, and each evening he and his staff performed fifteen to thirty abortions in the basement of his home. To avoid any emotional hangup, there was a psychiatrist in attendance. The minimum price was five hundred dollars; it soared into the thousands for celebrities.

The minimum recently went up to six hundred dollars — plumbers will do it for much less. Women who make appointments by telephone are usually instructed to drive into downtown Tijuana and park in the lot next to Woolworth's. A confidant will pick them up and circuitously drive them to the rendezvous. Some Mexican doctors with border-crossing cards will perform the abortion in your home if you can meet the price.

"The conditions under which abortions are performed in most cases are terribly primitive," says Bartelt. "We had a case not too long ago of a father who brought his daughter down to a small motel and went back across while the doctor performed the operation. Hours later he was instructed to pick up his girl at a different location. Well, he found her in a shack, dead. Meanwhile, the police had the place under surveillance and he was arrested. Imagine, finding your daughter dead in a place like that and then being thrown into the Tijuana jail. Of course, the abortionist got away. Police said they chased him and lost him, as they often do in these cases. The most recent case we had involved the wife of the sheriff of a northern California county."

The bail on an abortion charge (whether abortionist or abortionee) runs from eight hundred to two thousand dollars. Every year many Americans are fished up in the police net and hung to dry in the Tijuana jail (see Chapter 3).

Until New York changed its divorce laws, Juárez was the divorce capital of Mexico. Airline flights from Kennedy International Airport to El Paso were known as the "Divorce Run" or "Freedom Riders' Special."

"It was beautiful," a Mexican habitué of Juárez's plush Camino Real hotel told me. "Man, this place was the swingingest every night. *Ay*, these broads were sex maniacs. They'd just about rape you right at the bar. I've never had so much free stuff in my life. Everybody was making out." Times have changed, but Mexican *puñeteros* (cocksmen) are loath to admit it. The two nights I visited the bar at the Camino Real, there were at least a hundred men and not a single woman — not even a waitress.

Attorney Salvadore Franco Urias and two Juárez colleagues cooked up the Chihuahua divorce law in 1931, at the height of the depression. He called himself the Napoleon of the Mexican divorce industry, and kept a small bust of Napoleon on his desk. Later, with wealth, came a commitment to responsibility. He drifted south to a small state and was "elected" to the federal senate. But his contribution to air travel did not go unnoticed — he became an American Airlines vice-president and represented the company in Mexico.

Until recent years, all divorce negotiations were conducted by mail — a hundred percent proxy. Today, attorneys — not Mexican law — require the plaintiff to be present; the defendant signs a waiver. Exclusive of travel cost and lodging, a Juárez divorce will run from five hundred to a thousand dollars — over ninety percent to cover legal fees. The complaint, citing the most popular of twenty specified grounds, reads in part: "The reason our marriage failed is due to incompatibility of temperament and, therefore, we have had difficulties frequently until our life together became unbearable; we have last co-habited together some time ago."

Once the preliminary arrangements are completed by the American and Mexican attorneys, the plaintiff first goes to the second floor of the Juárez City Hall to sign the Official Registry of Residence. From there, he walks down the stairs and through a courtyard to one of the three divorce courts. If he is first in line, the procedure will take less than fifteen seconds. Formerly, some ten thousand people followed that route each year.

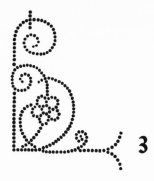

3

La Chícharra
and the
Little Monkey

I killed this guy, my sister's novio; *he was drunk and abusive and I put a knife into him. Then I went to the* cárcel *but right away the police accuse me of killing somebody else, some guy I didn't even know. The police here always try to pin everything they can on you, and if you don't confess, they torture you until you do. But I had already confessed to one killing, that was bad enough, so I denied everything, saying time and again, "No, no,* señor, *of that I am innocent." But nobody listened to me. "Okay, you son-of-a-whore," they kept saying, "so you're a real man, eh? Well, we'll see soon enough what kind of a man you are." And then wham! they would hit me again, in the face and against the head, while one cop behind me kept tapping my tailbone with his gun. I was dancing around with the pain even though I was very much against giving them the satisfaction. Later, when they realized I wasn't going to confess, they put me in a car and took me out to a canal where they made me undress and tied my hands and feet. It was night and very cold, with no moon or stars, pitch black except for their flashlights; but even then I could see that the water was filthy, you could smell the terrible stench; and for the first time I was very scared for my life. All of a sudden somebody tripped me, and down I went on my knees. Just then somebody punched me in the stomach, and before I could catch my breath, they pushed my head into the water and held it under until the water was rushing into my lungs and I knew I was going to drown. They call this the little drowning, el ahogadito. While this is going on, they hit me in the liver and kidneys, anyplace they could, all the time calling me bad names like son-of-a-whore, shit-head, and making fun of my manhood. At the end, when I didn't have the strength to resist anymore, and while my head was under water, they put the chicharra on my testicles and I passed out with the pain. Chicharra is what the police call the cattle prod, which sends electricity into your body. In Spanish, the word chicharra means cricket or talkative old woman, which is what you become when you get that treatment. To the cops it's the greatest invention since the rack. It's better than truth serum — it will teach you truths you never knew existed. Nobody can* resist it. It tears up your insides. I've seen prisoners who couldn't walk for days afterward. In some jails they hang you by your knees from a ceiling pipe, with your head down, throw a bucket of water on your naked body, and put the chicharra on your balls. It's called the little monkey. For some the pain is too great and their hearts give out, but it leaves no marks on the body, so you see nobody gets into trouble, right? They can make you confess to murdering your grandmother. I don't know why, but a Mexican cop always goes for your manhood. There's nothing he likes better than to hit you below the belt. I've seen guys with testicles swollen like grapefruits, and still they hit them. A man really wears pants, you know, muy macho, who can take that torture without cracking.

Me, I couldn't take it. All the way back to the jail that night I kept repeating "Sí, sí, señor" to everything they said. Still they weren't satisfied, for they beat me on the way back because of the trouble I had caused on the way out. When we arrived at the jail, they filled out an information sheet and took my fingerprints. I emptied my pockets and gave them my ring, watch and over seven hundred pesos for safekeeping because they said the prisoners would shake me down and take everything. But I never saw any of it again. It doesn't do any good to complain to officials, since the cops deny it and later really give it to you. You know, anybody who gets out of a Mexican jail is so happy to be free that he forgets his

grievances. Besides you never know when you'll fall into
their hands again, yes? . . .

Tijuana Mayor López was worried that Americans
would not respect Mexican law. "Many Americans," he
said, "think they only have to be respectful inside the
United States. They feel that when they cross into Mexico they are the owners of the roost. We have to teach
them it's a serious mistake. Otherwise, just imagine, there
would be no law outside the United States. That's not fair
to the rest of the world."

When I suggested the Tijuana jail be moved to the
border so that Americans crossing into Mexico would have
to walk through it, he fell back in his chair, laughing.
"Just movies would be enough," he said.

And, of course, he was right. The Tijuana jail is a
happening, and as such it would lend itself to photo-
graphic techniques, particularly Technicolor and Cinema-
scope. But to be fully appreciated it needs to be endured
by all the senses.

Built in 1946 during the interim administration of
Gonzalo Nava, the Tijuana jail is a modern facility by
border standards. "Oh, it was a very fine jail," Nava
recalled, "but the population of Tijuana was only about
thirty thousand then. Now it is maybe three hundred
thousand and the jail is a very bad place. I never go there
unless I have to help a friend, then I go to the police
station there at the jail, but never inside the jail. The
smell makes me ill. I think anybody with any sensitivity

would come out of there completely crazy after a week. I know Americans who have been in that jail, and they've never come back to Tijuana. And I can't say I blame them. Why even my own people, who are a little more used to hardship, are really scared of it."

"Boy," said a hardened customs agent, "it's tougher than hell, a real sonofabitch."

The American Consulate takes a more lenient attitude. "They don't treat Americans any worse than they do their own people," a vice-consul explained. "Besides, most Americans who land in jail bought what they get. They may say they only had one drink, but you know how it is. A lot of young kids, mostly servicemen, get drunk and raise holy hell. Hippies run around hopped up to the eyeballs; others are looking for abortions — all these things are as illegal here as they are in the United States. It's not the consulate's policy to storm the jails to rescue erring citizens. Everybody in Mexico must abide by Mexican law, including the consulate."

Accompanied by the consulate's protection officer, I visited the Tijuana jail — this began a practice that was to take me into nearly every bastille on the border, an experience not recommended for the squeamish. The first thing to assault the senses is the odor, so overpoweringly noxious that one fears it will leave a stain on his clothing. It is not only the putrescence of human waste, of sewage and gases, but a reeking blend of this and ages of decomposition, the decay of people and building, of mold and sweat and rust and fear and rot, a marasmus of steel and concrete, bringing forth a mephitic growth with a life of its own.

The jail is rectangular: three tiers, each with seven cells, face each other from opposite walls. In the well separating these walls is a steel staircase which leads to catwalks on each tier, and at both ends are large windows, the only source of natural light. The cells are small, perhaps seven by eight feet, with six bunks, three on each concrete sidewall, and in the concrete floor at the base of the back wall is a hole which serves as the water closet, except there is no water.

On the day of my visit, Americans occupied three cells — two for males and one for females. In the darkness of the windowless cells, it was difficult to make out the contorted bodies on the bunks — a rough head count revealed between seventeen and twenty in each cell. Several complained of having been mistreated, and two — they were charged with disorderly conduct — displayed ugly contusions on their bodies. The protection officer clucked his sympathy and promised to investigate the charges — later he mentioned it to the police, who raised heavy eyebrows and shook their heads in resignation: oh, the ingratitude of man. Others in the cells did not even look at the protection officer. They knew that his sole function was to notify their families, at their request. They lay in the bunks like broken mannequins, their limbs akimbo, determined to hold the precious space at all cost against the less fortunate who stood on the urine-soaked floor, their heads pressed against the sides of the bunks, the enormity of their problem making the weight of their heads insupportable. At least half of the prisoners were leftovers, losers who had failed to raise the fine or bail money, consigned now to their fate, to serving out their time. The ones facing more serious crimes would later be transferred to La Mesa state prison on the outskirts of Tijuana. There they would learn the true curse of poverty and the holiness of money.

Noise, the sheer unceasing weight of it, assaults the senses almost as violently as the odor: the harsh clang of metal against metal, of voices raised in anger and outrage, in anguish and defiance, in supplication and entreaty: "Ey, pleeze meester, give me a ceegareet, give me some mon-nee." In a ground-floor cell, a young Mexican girl, seated on a top bunk, leans back and pushes her legs through the bars, her bare feet curling on a cross bar, raising the lower part of her body to reveal the soft curves of her ilial crest, and slowly, methodically, dark eyes blank as she stares directly at her audience, begins to caress the inside of her thigh, her fingers moving tantalizingly to her exposed pubis. The prisoners privy to this performance shout their encouragement. Turnkeys grin fatuously as they rush about their mercenary duties. A fat policeman, asleep against a wall, barely raises puffed eyelids before nodding back into his own private nightmare. As she begins to masturbate, her eyes remain fixed ahead, but now the expression is one of defiance. The protection officer shakes his head and shrugs: "It's a crummy place, but nothing compared to La Mesa. Man, I wouldn't think of walking around in that prison like I do here. When I see a prisoner there, I have him brought to the warden's office." At that precise moment, a glob of excrement splashes at his feet. He jumps back, smiling nervously. "You've got to watch it around here. They're always throwing shit. They think it's funny as hell to smear you."

There were only a few women in the cell reserved for Americans on the third tier. All but one were asleep, and she was in no mood for small talk. The protection officer stared into the cell a long time before speaking. "Has Red heard from her family yet?" he said, pointing to a young girl (she appeared barely out of her teens) with long auburn hair, asleep now with her mouth open, her body compressed into a small ball — Baby Doll in the fetal position. The girl did not answer, did not even move her head. The protection officer opened his mouth but no words came out. He stared a while longer, then turned and walked away. "She's angry as a hornet," he said, leading the way on the narrow catwalk toward the stairs. "She thinks the consulate is a finance company. They can be stupid at times, you know. Red is okay, though. She's my favorite around here, but she's got a real problem. Abortion rap. She was still on the table when the cops broke in. Unless her family comes up with sixteen hundred dollars pretty quick she's going to be transferred to La Mesa. I'm afraid they don't realize how tough it is out there."

If there's any place in God's creation where money is essential to survival, it's in a Mexican prison. Without it you're doomed. There's no way one can exaggerate the importance of money or the calculated cruelty of prison life. The prisoners are even more greedy than the guards. They'll tear the clothes right off your back, take your shoes and sell them to buy food or marijuana, all of which is as nothing compared to some of the other things that go on in there. Everyone in Mexico has heard of these cruelties, but no one can really imagine how horrible it is unless he has seen it for himself. There's a price for everything: four hundred pesos for a bed, which is just a board on blocks to get it off the floor, a hundred and twenty-five pesos for an old greasy blanket that smells like it was washed in the toilet, one peso for a shower, ten pesos every eight days for the talacha, which is the cleanup by prisoners who can't afford to pay it. They have brigades of these guys constantly going around mopping up, but they really only move the dirt around from one place to another. If you can't pay this money, they put you in a tank where all the poor, withering people are, with no beds, no blankets, no water, no toilet, no windows, no floor, just dirt; they dig a hole in the corner and use that for a toilet, and the flies and cockroaches are so thick you can hardly see the people. At night rats the size of a perro de presa (bulldog) run around in there like crazy. These people don't have any utensils to eat with except maybe an old tin can or pop bottle, and, of course, their hands, which they dip into the big cans they use to serve the foul slop they have the nerve to call food. If one guy gets a piece of cardboard to sleep on and somebody steals it, they may fight to the death over it with knives or any other weapon *available. Mostly they die of dysentery, tuberculosis, pneumonia, all the diseases caused by bad food and exposure to the elements. Of course, there's a lot of syphilis and other kinds of venereal disease, guys in terrible stages of decay, some even, I think, with leprosy. . . .*

Mexican prisons are not always tough. On the contrary, they can be made quite soft for a prisoner with unlimited funds — like Val Culwell, a former Los Angeles automobile dealer, who only a few years ago had gained some prominence as the Smiling Irishman on the late-late show. Culwell was first sentenced in 1965 to five years and eight months for passing counterfeit money. In 1967 he was sentenced to an additional seven years (terms never run concurrently in Mexico) for grand larceny and conspiracy — to wit, having operated an international auto-theft ring from the premises of La Mesa prison itself — a feat certainly as ingenious as any featured in the potboilers he sponsored on television.

Upon first entering La Mesa in 1965, Culwell purchased a fourteen-foot house trailer from the warden, and with it the privilege of parking it in an enclosed area outside the main prison compound. The trailer included all the modern conveniences, plus guest privileges for both his wife and girlfriend (Idonna Fern O'Blennis, with the alias of Idonna West) for periods of days at a time. When the FBI persuaded the Mexican federal police to crack down on Culwell's auto-theft ring, Idonna became a permanent guest at La Mesa. Her role in the ring's operation was to transport stolen automobiles, mostly Lincolns and Cadillacs, across the border to the prison yard at La Mesa, where Culwell and a crew of inmates made certain alterations. Forged documents were provided and the cars were either driven back across the border or south into the interior of Mexico.

La Mesa prison, which occupies approximately ten acres, is enclosed by a high wall of gray concrete blocks. The warden's office is to the immediate left of the main entrance and the women's tank to the right. Both are protected from the prison compound by a wire fence — this was the area where Culwell's trailer had been parked before his conviction on the auto-theft charge. The old warden has since retired, and according to authorities, reforms have been instituted.

On my visit to La Mesa, Culwell came to meet me in the warden's office. As he came into the room, I was standing at a window, looking out in the prison yard at a scene often simulated in war movies to depict the obscene misery of a Japanese prisoner-of-war camp. I turned and there he stood in all his groomed splendor: clear blue eyes, hair combed neatly, clean-shaven, robust and cheerful, sport shirt and slacks immaculate, alligator shoes a mirror of his gleaming survival. It was like walking into Changi and coming face to face with King Rat.

"You're a writer, eh?" he said, his beefy hand closing over mine in a paralyzing grip. "Well, I'll bet I can tell you a thing or two." His laugh was as fierce as his grip. "C'mon, let's go to my pad and talk." He strode from the office and out through the gate in the wire fence, into the prison yard where men in rags and flies in clusters broke in waves before him. Hands pulled frantically at my clothes as voices beseeched alms. "Don't listen to 'em," he shouted. "You pull out money here and they'll tear you to pieces like mad dogs." I smiled sympathetically, as warmly as I could under the circumstances, and trotted desperately in the vacuum of his stride.

His pad turned out to be a little bungalow, a *caraca* as he called it, at the far end of the prison yard. He opened the screen door and waved me inside. A man lay asleep on a double bed with a small white terrier at his side. "Hey, White Trash!" he bellowed, pulling roughly at the sleeping man's leg. "Out!" White Trash, also an American, stumbled out, rubbing sleep from his eyes, his elbows poking sharply through large holes in his sweater.

"Make yourself at home," he said, indicating a chair near the bed. The dog raised its head, tail wagging. "That's Savage," he said, picking up the dog. "Weighs two kilos. Can I fix you something? Like a diet cola? Sorry, can't offer you anything stronger. Never drank or smoked in my life. Always been a health fiend. I used to play ball with the Giants, football, a few years ago; did you know that? But I weighed two-forty then — I've lost thirty pounds."

As he talked I surveyed the room in stunned silence. Besides the double bed, which was covered by a chenille bedspread, white with a pink flower design, there was a refrigerator on top of which sat a twenty-one-inch television set, a kitchen cabinet with a hot plate, a pressure cooker, dishes, pots and pans, cooking utensils, silverware, including a large butcher knife, two chairs, a closet with clothes hanging neatly from a pipe rack, a five-gallon bottle of spring water on a stand, assorted lamps, linoleum on the floor and wallpaper on the walls. On two of the walls were shelves loaded down with American canned goods: peaches, pears, peas, stringbeans, tomatoes, in quantity and variety to make any housewife envious.

"Hey, White Trash!" The screen door opened and White Trash tentatively poked his head inside. Culwell made a motion with his head and thumb toward the closet. White Trash smiled, his eyes never leaving mine as he scurried to the closet, reached in with one hand, retrieved a white chamberpot, and scurried out again, the screen door banging shut behind him.

"We're a little shy on toilet facilities around here," Culwell said, in explanation. "In fact, this place is a little shy on a lot of things. When I first came here I lived up front, beyond the wire fence, next to the warden's office. I lived there in a nice trailer for eighteen months. It wasn't really like being in prison. Well, this is not bad, either. I suppose if a guy has to be in prison, he could do worse than here. I might add it helps if you have a little bit of money. I'm a federal prisoner and all they give me is a *cheavo*, which is twenty-eight cents a day to live on. The state prisoners get to eat off the line. In the morning they get a watered-down mush that looks just awful; at lunch it's some atrocious soup, the stink is enough to knock you out, and at night it's beans, half done — *frijoles*, what we call pinto beans. The same menu every day, seven days a week. A *cheavo* buys nothing in this place. They've got a restaurant here and it's the filthiest place in this prison and still you can't get anything in there for less than a buck. I cook all my meals, unless there's a shakedown. The guards here don't bother you too much, it's those bastards from downtown. You've got to hide everything, eyeglasses, pills — I've got sugar diabetes, Christ, they'd take your crutches if you were an amputee. They strip the place clean, all the canned goods, everything goes. Of course, they'll sell it all back to you at a discount.

"Otherwise, things are fairly calm around here. We have what they call *lista*, roll call, in the morning and evening. It's never at the same time. One morning it's at seven, the next at seven-thirty, eight, six — Mexicans never do anything on schedule or by a timetable. They never do anything the same way twice. The guard might be up there on the wall today, and then he might not be there again for two weeks. One night they make me turn off the television at ten, the next night they come in at twelve and want to watch it with me. After *lista*, you're on your own. Well, some of the prisoners have odd jobs, but there's no regular program. There's only one thing everybody understands around here, and that's money. They even charge you a dollar a week for showers, and the water's filthy.

"But I don't mind that. What really bugs me around here are the courts, they're something else. By the time

you tell your side of the story to an interpreter and he tells
it to the judge's secretary who tells it to a typist, by the
time it comes back to you in translation, it sounds like a
different case. Hell, man, they weren't talking about me
in that court, it was three other guys. You know, I never
even saw the judge. Everything was handled by the secretary." What about graft? Did they try to get money from
you? "You better believe it. They don't only try, they do.
Attorneys, in my opinion, are bad all over the world, but
here in Mexico they are twenty times worse than in the
states. They string you along and bleed you dry. They're
the promisingest people in the world. Man, they'd promise you that the gallows rope would break if it meant a
couple more bucks of *mordida*. They work hand in hand
with the cops. The minute they've got you locked up they
knock their heads together and try to figure how much
shakedown you're good for. I went through fifteen attorneys before I found one with a heart. Now I'm going to
win this case. After three years, after they've taken all my
money, most of my teeth, my health, I'm going to be
proven not guilty. Well, I'll be happy to get out, real
happy.

"You see that stolen-car business was a lot of bullshit, a
figment of people's imaginations. The only thing stolen
was the twenty-one cars they stole from me. I've been in
the car business all my life. I was the biggest dealer in
Southern California. I was the Smiling Irishman, I spent a
thousand dollars a day on advertising. I gave my own
commercials on television. They came out here and

searched my trailer and claimed they found pink slips and license plates from Texas and all kinds of crap. They found nothing. There's two sides to every story, three sides sometimes, or maybe seven sides. But here there's only one side. But what can you expect from a town like Tijuana, where the main industry is dope. It means lots and lots of bad deals. So here I am in this place, fighting the system with the only thing I know they understand: money. Meanwhile, I've got to watch my back every minute. Man, they've got guys in here who'd chop you up for meat if they could sell the *tacos*. This place is loaded with killers and hypes, guys who have nothing to lose no matter what the hell they do. There's no capital punishment, so what difference does it make how many scalps they get, and there are guys here who have maybe fifty, maybe more, who knows. Real bad people. And at night you've got the rats to contend with. They're big enough to swallow you alive." He stops and tickles Savage under the ear. "He's my bodyguard. Fearless little bastard. You want junk or pot? There's a place right next to the soft-drink stand, sell you all you want, hand it right out the window like candy. To hear these Mexicans talk you'd think the United States was the only place with a narcotics problem. Well, take it from me, they've got a big one here, too. And I don't mean just in this prison, either. Hell, man, pot is as common here as Camels in the States. Everybody smokes it."

The worst thing of all is the sex life. Ay, it is a catastrophe. They will jump a guy and while they hold him by the neck with his arms pinned behind his back, a dozen guys will take turns screwing him. Then he's told to keep his mouth shut or they'll kill him. When a young kid comes in for the first time, some gang leader will grab him right away and say he's mine, for always. He says if anybody messes with him, he'll stick a knife in them. Later, after his lust is satisfied, he sells him like a pimp with a whore. Even guys who have wives coming every week for the conjugal visit take part in these homosexual rapes. And the women prisoners, Ay, desastrada. When a young girl comes in, it doesn't matter if she's married or not, a guard will screw her first; if she's pretty, the captain will take her on himself. If she objects, she's stripped naked and thrown into the separo, which is a small room, no bigger than a closet, with steel walls and water dripping in, and no light except for a tiny slit in the steel door. In no time she's crying her head off to get out, promising to do anything anybody wants. In most Mexican prisons, the men and women are separated only by a wire fence, and when a prisoner sees a woman he wants, he makes a deal with one of the turnkeys, who are bums, you know, crooks, who work in prisons all over Mexico for nothing; that is, without pay, but they make plenty from the prisoners, which they split with the officials. A turnkey can get you anything for a price. They bring in the dope, booze, knives, anything you can afford. For ten pesos, or whatever the turnkey can get, he will take the woman to a little room, and stand there like a ticket collector at the door while maybe a whole line of guys wait their turn. A

woman will get screwed more times in one year in prison
than she will all the rest of her life. . . .

"Our laws are different from yours," says Mayor López.
"According to our constitution, a woman can be a prostitute, and it is not a crime. It is a crime to have prostitutes
working for you, you understand — to exploit them, that's
a crime. If a woman is a prostitute, you can't even put her
in jail. It's true that there are houses with pimps and all
that, but they work like that because otherwise we would
have a very much bigger problem. You see, we are more
advanced than the United States in this respect, more
sophisticated, you might say. We allow prisoners to receive what you call the conjugal visit, and you see that
stops all this homosexual business you have in your prisons
in the United States. Our principles are different, beginning in our homes and our families. We are not as free as
you are, we might say, with your women. But we allow
prostitution, and it's according to our law, and you don't.
You have higher sex crimes than we do, maybe a thousand
to one, I don't know. When we figured that out, we
decided we would rather have prostitution than this kind
of crime. You are the other way around. You'd rather have
those crimes and try to stop prostitution."

White Trash was waiting for me when I came out of
Culwell's *caraca*. "I threw my whole life away in five
minutes," he cried, clutching desperately at my arm. "I
got real drunk here one night at the races and some

animal took advantage of me in the john, and I killed him. Just like that. Five minutes, and I blew my whole life. I was a drummer with a band in Hollywood, and I've traveled all over the United States as a musician, and never once got in trouble. Five lousy minutes." Suddenly tears were streaming down his cheeks. "I've been here six years." He stopped and pointed at Culwell. "This man saved my life. Without him . . ." he lowered his head, choked with emotions, unable to continue. "White Trash is okay," Culwell said. "He wouldn't harm a fly. Like a lot of guys around here, he's had a raw deal."

In seconds we were inundated in a sea of hands reaching clawlike toward us: "mon-nee, mon-nee, pleeze, mon-nee, meester. . . ." "Jesus," said Culwell. "They've got you pegged as a rich gringo. Hey, c'mon, break it up," he shouted. "Move it!" But they stood their ground, their plea rising like a chant. The rescue was effected by the deputy warden, Tony Martínez, a tall, thin man with a dapper moustache and receding chin. He took my arm and wheeled me through the crowd, his face grimly set as he kept repeating, "*Vato!*" in a soft but firm voice.

Later, on a tour of the prison, Martínez showed me the cellblocks where the less-fortunate prisoners (the overwhelming majority) were lodged: long, narrow, windowless sheds with double tiers of cells the size of burial vaults. Hot and fetid with the same stench as the Tijuana jail, illuminated by a single bare bulb, the cellblock constitutes a Mexican tradition in penology being almost identical in construction and condition along the entire border — even to the makeshift cardboard screens devised for privacy by prisoners receiving conjugal visits from wives, consorts or whores. The cellblocks are individually fenced in, within the fenced-in compound, within the fenced-in prison.

Here, as elsewhere in Mexico, children played in the prison yard, offspring of motherless homes now in the custody of convict fathers, sharing the meager food, over-crowding, corruption and bestiality of prison life. In some prisons, entire families move in and set up housekeeping in cellblocks. In a culture where children are rarely punished, where the favorite toy is a baby, where bourgeois fathers proudly display their children on Sunday, this is a brutal paradox. But Mexico is a land of wild contradictions, of perplexing paradoxes, strange and mysterious and sometimes surprisingly heartwarming — but that is another story.

A Mexican prison is more than the sum total of bad food and bad sanitation. It is built along the lines of a concentration camp, not a house of correction. The tortures practiced within are comparable only to those of medieval dungeons, with electricity having replaced the versatility of the wheel. The brutality of prison guards and convict gangs is the accepted norm of behavior. Narcotics and liquor are peddled and used openly, and sexual perversion flourishes despite conjugal visits.

One of the reasons for so much violence within the prison is the violence without. The nation's per capita homicide rate is one of the (if not *the* highest in the world: approximately thirty-five murders per hundred thousand population annually as compared to less than five in the United States. The state of Guerrero, with Acapulco as its largest city, averages two hundred murders a month. Acapulco, with a population far under one hundred thousand, averages sixty murders a month, which is more than New York City, including all boroughs and Kings, Nassau, Rockland, Suffolk and Westchester counties, a total population of some eleven million.

Guns blaze quickly in Mexico. Affronts to one's character, however dubious, are not taken lightly. And once a gun blazes, others join in the chorus. A Mexican with a gun deserves all the respect his temperament indicates. This is particularly important to remember in the tropical coastal zones, where the homicide rate soars to a whopping 100.2 per hundred thousand. All of this, of course, is quite romantic, and forms the basis for the nation's popular music — lyrics dwell lugubriously on the mystique of sudden death and imprisonment — and comprises the entire repertoire of the *mariachis*.

The high homicide rate and the national aversion to capital punishment has made for a prison clientele with a colorful expertise in violence. There are no statistics (a rare commodity in Mexico) on the murder rate in prisons, but the mere concentration of so much talent must make the atmosphere endemic — the numerical results would certainly boggle the mind of American penologists.

The system being what it is, many prisoners have given up hope. They don't care anymore about people or even themselves. They live like animals, and so they behave like animals. The greed in their eyes shines like a madness. They kill each other for a piece of bread. There are prisoners who have committed so many murders they don't even know themselves how many. A hundred, maybe even more. The tank they threw me into was one of the worst there, with killers and dope fiends and homosexuals who are always grabbing at you. The moment I came in, somebody noticed the mark on my finger left by the ring I had turned over to the guards, and they started beating me because they thought I was hiding it.

The head man in this tank was a prisoner by the name of Daniel Maron, a member of a big family of dope smugglers, very wild and tough people, with quite a few of them having been killed by the police. Daniel himself was in for having killed the chief of police. His reputation was one of muy macho. It was to my good fortune that he recognized me almost instantly. Once he had stored several tons of marijuana on my father's ranch. So right away he took me under his wing. He gave me a knife and said, "Okay, pal, there ain't nobody gonna mess with you." Then he told everybody to lay off. My father brought me money every week, and I ate all my meals in the prison restaurant. My father knew all about the food and conditions there because he had served nearly a year for killing two guys. I was sentenced to six years, but my father paid five thousand pesos to a judge to disagree with the sentence; it was reduced to two years. Then my father paid ten thousand pesos for a bond and I was released after eight months. Also I have to pay fifteen hundred pesos to a

*court official, who the judge made responsible for me. If I
don't pay him, he can get the bond canceled and have me
thrown back in jail. . . .*

Tijuana is one of the few bordertowns which has both
a precinct jail and a state penitentiary. Most places make
do with a multipurpose bastille, mixing murderers, dope
peddlers, rapists and robbers with teen-agers recovering
from a first binge and traffic violators still puzzled by the
word *alto*. It makes for a salutary experience.

The oldest prison is in Matamoros, across the border
from Brownsville, Texas. In the opinion of a consulate
officer, "It is the filthiest, dirtiest, stinkiest place on the
face of the earth. I've been through South America, Asia,
where's there's incredible poverty, but this is something
out of the dark ages. They don't have cells, but huge
bullpens, completely bare, dirt floor, and they keep dump-
ing the prisoners in until there's hardly room for anyone
to lie down. There's no water or toilet facilities. They just
go in the corner, and when the pile gets big enough,
somebody goes in with a wheelbarrow and shovels it out.
Then there are the flies and cockroaches and rats, not to
mention the criminals dumped into these bullpens.
When a man is in a cell with six others, he's got six
chances of getting worked over. In a bullpen with four
hundred, I say he's in deep trouble. The food is vile, and
there's no utensils to eat with — most of them eat with
their hands. I can tell you that we do our damnedest to
get Americans out as quickly as humanly possible. One of

the most frequent problems for tourists is automobile accidents. I don't think there's anyone more dangerous behind a steering wheel than a Mexican. They drive like kamikaze pilots. It all has to do with *machismo*, their obsession with masculinity, their walk-through-hell-itself-before-ignoring-an-insult brand of courage. Even the most unassuming Mexican thinks of himself as *muy macho*, you know, plenty man, with very strong overtones of reckless pride. It has something to do with latent homosexuality and frail egos, I'm told. Perhaps a little more complex, but basically sound. It accounts for most of the violence. Some historians have conjectured that, since Cortés, more Mexicans have died violently than quietly. It may be true. At any rate, a Mexican in an automobile can only be described as a motorized phallus in search of conquest. He is not like the economy-minded Frenchman trying to save time. The Mexican is concerned with *his* honor, *his* pride, *his* virility. He will not be cuckolded by anyone or anything, especially a gringo or a fat American car. On the other hand, the gringo is automatically in the wrong, even if the Mexican drives him up a tree. Being an American is one strike against him immediately. If he can't speak Spanish, that's two strikes; and if he doesn't have Mexican insurance, he's definitely out. An automobile accident in Mexico is a crime against the state, and it doesn't matter who's right or wrong. Everybody goes to jail until the court places the responsibility."

The assistant police chief in Piedras Negras was stomped to death by prisoners. His favorite interrogative technique was to make a naked prisoner stand in a pail of water while he persuaded him with the *chicharra*.

"Mexican police get a confession one way or another," said a customs agent in Laredo. "They'll take a man in the dead of winter, put him in a cell naked, and every thirty minutes toss a bucket of water on him. Or they'll hold his hand or foot on an electric grill, or use the cattle prod. I've known them to take a prisoner to the cemetery late at night, have him dig a grave, throw him in it, and start shoveling dirt in his face. The point is, right or wrong, you're going to confess. But if you've got money coming in, you can get a private cell and fix it up like your room at home. There's no limit to the comforts and pleasures you can buy."

"Once when I was in the office of the chief of Mexican Customs in Chihuahua," an American official recalled, "he invited me to accompany him while he interrogated a prisoner. We went into a room, not far from his office, and he unlocked a solid steel grate in the floor and slid it open. And there, crouched in a small hole in the ground, was a man, wallowing in his own filth, his hair and beard slick with slime, his eyes those of a madman. I turned and walked out, out of the room and out of the building. I'm sure my abrupt departure puzzled the chief greatly — the whole business is so routine."

Refugio "Puco" Rubialcava is the assistant state police chief in Juárez. His office is in the Juárez jail, a gray medieval fortress with an inmate population four times its capacity. He is short, sandy-haired, clean-cut and expensively dressed. He looks enough like singer Mel Torme to pass as a twin brother if he were older. He is the last person one expects to find seated behind a battered desk in that battered jailhouse office. He is charmingly and warmly personable as he explains in softly accented English that a tour of the prison is unthinkable, the dangers lurking therein far too unpredictable. So with the help of small ladders and long planks, we climbed to the top of the administration building and looked down into the bleak prison yard and at the cellblocks converging into it. As before, the design is that of a concentration camp. It is the dinner hour, and two prisoners stagger out of a small shack, lugging a huge garbage can between them — it is the night's meal. A cloud of flies forms a solid lid over the can.

"Hey," says the American officer who introduced me to Rubialcava, "know why God put wings on flies?"

"No."

"So they could beat Mexicans to the garbage can."

The officer, who is a Mexican-American, punches Rubialcava affectionately on the arm, who smiles and punches back.

"Know why Mexicans wear pointed shoes?"

"No."

"To kill the cockroaches in the corners." Rubialcava continues to smile. It is evident he has heard all of this before.

"Know why they don't kill flies in Mexico?"

"No."

"It's the national bird."

The prisoners gather around the can and begin dipping into the watery contents with makeshift utensils.

"As you can see," says Rubialcava, "the food doesn't look too appetizing; but most prisoners get extra food from their families. Our big problem right now is that the state prison in Chihuahua refuses to accept any more prisoners. That's why we're so overcrowded. Otherwise, the conditions here are pretty good. Our funds are limited, but we do the best we can for these poor people."

"It's the best cure for alcoholism I know of," says Marshall Hail. "One night in the Juárez jail, and you'll swear off for life. You'd never believe it by looking at it, but this is a new jail. It's only about twenty years old. The old jail had dirt floors and most of it was uncovered. Prisoners literally froze to death. I remember a Mexican newspaperman, he was editor of *El Alacrán,* who made the mistake of criticizing an official and was shot in the leg for his trouble. They threw him in jail, and I went to see him one day and found the poor guy sitting on the bare ground in one of the uncovered bullpens, suffering terribly, his wounded leg wrapped in filthy bandages — the outer bandage was an old piece of burlap. He was kept in jail without trial, and that was the last I ever heard of him. This sort of thing still happens, particularly among poor people who have no legal recourse. They're at the mercy of the authorities. Mexican law is based on Roman law and the code of Napoleon, which makes it very hard on its people. You're guilty until proven innocent, and the burden of proof is on you."

Aureliano González Vargas, a prominent attorney and a

former mayor of Juárez, gets annoyed at the misconceptions Americans have about Mexican law: "We have a bill of rights in our constitution, the same as you do. We have very specific individual guarantees set forth and established in articles fourteen and sixteen of the supreme court. Misconceptions about people being guilty until proven innocent arise from the fact that generally defense attorneys, instead of sitting back and letting the prosecutor prove a person's guilt, will go out of their way to prove his innocence. It has become a habit. Mexicans have all the rights and guarantees that Americans do: the police can't search a person's home without probable cause and a court order; upon arrest a person has the right of counsel and can't be held incommunicado. One difference, we don't believe in jury trials, except in cases involving treason or crimes committed by federal employees in the exercise of their duties. The general opinion in Mexico is that juries tend to be swayed by emotions rather than by fact or the truth. Of course, Mexican judges sometimes tend to be overly sentimental." (*Delitto d' onore*, the crime of honor, which dates back to 400 B.C. in Italy, is even more rigidly enforced in Mexico: husbands who kill unfaithful wives are never convicted.) "However, we do have two legal rights you don't have in the United States. One is the bond system, which allows a person convicted of a crime to post a bond if the sentence is for five years or less. And the other is the *amparo*, which is a writ issued by a judge to anyone who feels he will be unjustly accused of a crime. No arrest can be made of this person as long as he holds an *amparo*. Or a person convicted in one court can get an *amparo* in another court to stop the first court from executing its sentence. The *amparo* can protect a person even against the wishes of the president. Unfortunately, there has been much abuse of this privilege, even to the point of some crooks getting an *amparo* before they go out to commit a crime." But what if a person cannot afford a bond, or an *amparo,* or even the services of an attorney? "Well, of course, in that case the police will protect his rights. We don't have a public-defender system in Mexico as yet, but we are making much progress in this direction. In fact, we are making progress in every direction, every day."

In those eight months, I was beaten many times by the police. Never did I know why. I guess they just do it from habit. I guess when a policeman wants to know something, you don't go into the philosophy of why he wants to know. He's a policeman, and he's going to find out if it kills you. Their idea of investigation is to get a lot of goats and heat them up. "Come," they say, "it's getting cold out; it's time for a little heating up. Sing and cough up a few saints." All I can say is that it's a filthy business. The police here are organized like your gangsters in the United States. They are the biggest crooks in the country; they can get away with anything, and believe me they do. I know this must sound unpatriotic but it's true — there's no justice in my country. There's only the power of money. If you don't have it, you're at the mercy of the police, and there's nothing you can do about it. I'm a Mexican, and it shames me to say this, but my people have no heart, no compassion for the poor creature who is down and out. They won't lift a finger to help him, but many will go out of their way to step on his head and push him down lower. Innocent men literally rot in prison because they lack the few pesos for a payoff, while criminals live in big houses and are saluted by the police. I know about the system. I killed a man and served only eight months, but maybe I'll pay the mordida *for the rest of my life. My father killed two unarmed men during an argument and served less than a year. What better proof is there to the disgrace and shame of our justice. . . .*

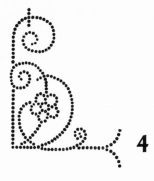

4

The Politics
of *Mordída*

Mexican politicians have two national unifying forces: *El Presidente*, who symbolizes the revolutionary mystique of PRI (Partido Revolucionario Institucional — the ruling political party), and *la mordida*, the bite, which makes the flame of politics worthy of the candle.

To businessmen along the border, *mordida* is the biggest word in Mexico. It is not simple graft, but a corrosive blend of bribery and extortion. Another big word is *palanca*, which in the idiom means pull — to have influence and connections. A man with *palanca*, if he is rich, is called a *pezgordo*, a fat fish. A *pezgordo* never pays the little *mordida* to police, customs or local officials. Subordinates are only too happy to serve him, because he is a

man of substance, and such a man is much respected —
and feared. (Regardless of a man's position, be it mayor,
governor or minister, the title that precedes his name on
all documents and identification paraphernalia is his university degree — *Lic.* for *licenciado, Ing.* for *ingeniero,*
etc. — a custom popular in underdeveloped nations where
education is still the ultimate status symbol.)

Roberto Moya is a nightclub impresario in Juárez. He
has wealth, but he is definitely not a *pezgordo.* His
palanca is purchased hourly on the installment plan. His
venture into the entertainment field came by accident:
"My brother and I bought a corner on Juárez Avenue to
install a supermarket — curios and liquor — and there was
this club, The Follies, a strip show, so we operated it
while getting ready to open the store. Well, business was
so good we decided to sell the supermarket and run the
club. Later we picked up five more clubs. But now we'd
like to sell them and go into some other kind of business.
Too much *mordida,* too much trouble with the unions,
too much taxes. We pay the state tax every month, they
tell you how much you have to pay; the city tax also every
month, plus special assessments whenever they feel like it;
then there's the annual federal income tax, and whether
you make a good or bad declaration, they never like it —
you have to pay the *mordida* or they put any big amount
they want to on your return. The sanitary inspectors get a
payoff every time they come in the place. They don't even
look at the show, but if you give them something, they
like it right away. Then we have many different police

forces working independently in the city. There's the bilingual police, who work the main streets to help tourists; the secret police, which is the detective bureau; *veladors*, night watchmen paid by the city; the *patrullas*, which is the patrol unit; the state police; the federal police; and the federal judicial police, who work all kinds of cases, especially narcotics. Also there's the special police and the mayor's inspectors. All these forces keep checking the shows and collecting the *mordida*. Then we have customs agents who check the liquor and cigarettes and fixtures, everything, for possible contraband, and they get the *mordida*.

"By law, to have a strike in Mexico, a majority of all the people who work in a place have to vote for it. But the unions are so powerful in Mexico City that when they want a new contract all they have to do is tell you to sign; if you refuse, they close you up. When the union decided to double the wages of strippers, the majority was on our side, so we refused to sign. One day before the strike was to be called, we were brought into the mayor's office and he said, 'I don't want any trouble in Mexico City and I don't want any trouble in Juárez. You sign this contract or I will close all your clubs.' So we signed. It's just that simple in this type of business. You pay and you obey. That's why we're going out of the nightclub business."

The *mordida* system is so deeply ingrained into the national economy that guidebook writers feel a need to comment on it. In his *Bachelor's Mexico*, Boye De Mente notes that "Mexican police are inclined to be lenient with

Americans . . . but this does not mean the visitor can ignore or forget the 'pay-off' system. On the contrary, the police expect more from Americans for the logical reason that Americans have more. High-level statements in the press that the age-old system of *mordida* has been eliminated from Mexico, are mere diplomacy. The entire economy of the country is greased by the system. If one encounters official resistance in any form or runs afoul of the law in a relatively minor way, the best idea is to forget principle, find out as quickly and subtly as possible how much will do the job, fork it over and be on your way."

J. Paul Hightower's *Bluebook Guide to Mexico* refers to it in a section on tipping. "The usual tip is . . . ten pesos to the inspector who examines your luggage and ten more pesos to the man who writes your permit for automobile entry. This is not compulsory but it will facilitate matters to get you through the red tape quicker and a pack of cigarettes as additional bonus will get fast action."

Even the incomparable Kate Simon presents it in terms of a gratuity. In *Mexico: Places and Pleasures*, she writes: "As it does everywhere else, money talks in Mexico, but rather more simply and openly than in other places. Salaries are so low (a traffic policeman earns about two dollars a day) that bribes are generally counted on as part of a salary, comparable to a waiter's tips. Going to Acapulco by plane in season can be arranged by sweetening a hand (the more realistic Mexican calls it the bite, *la mordida*). Customs men can be moved, so can policemen, so can people in government offices. A *mordida* can whistle lost papers out of their hiding place and act like a magic wand when words, gestures, and the attrition of passing time have no effect. . . . The present situation has its clear uses to the traveler, however. For a little money, he can save himself hours and days of time, the services of an interpreter and, in addition, feel considerably more powerful than he might in the same situation at home."

José Gorduno, publisher of Tijuana's *Las Noticias*, brings a more realistic attitude to the problem. "The policemen here," he says, "don't make very much a month, so they are looking around to see where they can get an extra buck from somebody. What they are doing is picking up people on the street, whether they have done something wrong or not. If they don't pay the *mordida*, the cops run them in and say they were resisting arrest, or some damn lie, and it will cost them twenty-four dollars or fifteen days in jail. There's been so much graft here, so much exploitation of vice and prostitution, that Americans are not coming in the same numbers they used to; even if it is flourishing, it is still smaller than before. And the reason for this is the crooked cops and pimps who work the whorehouses and bars. They are so greedy that they steal the money from the people, and if they complain, they get beaten up. These people tell their friends not to come to Tijuana. This means that the governor and mayor and the politicians and policemen are making less graft money on vice than they used to."

José Gorduno has been fighting the vice-*mordida* system since he began publishing in 1945. Twice he was framed and both times escaped by the skin of his teeth. In 1948, he says, seven cans of opium were planted in his car, and he was kept in jail four days before a federal judge ordered his release. Two years later, fourteen cans of opium were found in his car, and this time he spent eleven days in jail before a judge again released him. "People say I was lucky," he says. "They thought I was going to get killed for my attacks against politicians. We had a very bad bunch of crooks in office and lots of people disappeared at that time. That was before we had statehood. The governor was appointed in Mexico City, and these people would come in from out of state with their henchmen and steal everything they could, leaving nothing for the cities or the people. When we made the change to statehood and elected our first governor, Braulio Maldonado, we thought we had put a stop to that. But we found out that we were badly mistaken, because Maldonado was one of the worst thieves we ever had here. Maldonado is supposed to be a Communist, but I don't believe that. I don't think we have any *real* Communists here in Mexico. It's like one of our presidents said one time: 'There's not a general who can withstand a broadside of fifty thousand pesos.' The same applies to Communists. All they care is how much they can make for themselves. Maldonado was the one who burned and bulldozed the squatters out of the riverbed because he hoped to build that big canal with the United States and make a whole bunch of money. But it didn't work out that way. It made such a big scandal that Mexico City put a stop to it. Besides being after money all the time, politicians here are always thinking of the next office they want to hold. This is a hell of a way to do things. Mayor López here talks about being governor. Meanwhile, he's got a construction company, and he's presently doing a lot of construction for the city. He's also a big gambler and spends a lot of time in Las Vegas."

"My father was in real estate," says Mayor López, "but when I took over I got interested in construction. I had interest in company and then I buy it out. I like more the construction company than real estate, so I change my interest to construction, because here, you know, that is the biggest industry. Yes, Las Vegas, I like very much. It is good place to have good fun, yes; and you know they are very nice there to public officials. But, unfortunately, I don't have time to go there too much, for we are very busy here all the time."

Back in 1956, when Tijuana had a population of sixty-five thousand, and Avenida Revolución could boast of more joints than Bubbling Well Road in prewar Shanghai, Manuel Acosta Meza raised considerable hell for a brief period. First as editor of *ABC*, one of five dailies, which was soon purchased by a group of local cabaret owners, and then as a columnist for *El Imparcial*, a weekly, Acosta Meza launched a bitter attack against politicians and hoodlums involved in prostitution and vice rackets. His crusade lasted less than four months before an unknown assassin shot him dead. Governor Maldonado was quoted as being "horrified" by the murder, and the Tijuana police chief resigned. His replacement noted that his men were underpaid, but that "I will get an ax and cut all the dead limbs from this tree." Forty of the seventy known brothels closed for a few hours.

Aurelio García, a Tijuana stringer for the San Diego *Union,* knew Acosta Meza: "He started crusading for this and that, when at one time he had been involved with the same people. That's Chicago stuff, that doesn't go, they get it sooner or later. I've been writing here for many years and nothing has ever happened to me. But if I strayed over certain bounds and limitations that we all have — I mean, if you call a crook a crook to his face, he is bound to sock you in the puss."

"One of Maldonado's cousins had him killed," says Gorduno. "Everybody in Tijuana knew it. The cousin had this newspaper, and he gave Acosta Meza fifteen thousand dollars to run it. Well, he started to knock the governor, and then went after the cousin, who was the governor's bagman for the vice operation. When Acosta Meza refused to resign, they sold the paper; but then he got another job, and they got tired of fooling around with him."

In 1963, Carlos Esprada Sastre was murdered under similar circumstances. "Esprada Sastre was a politician who came to Baja to profit from his ties with politicians who were then in power," says Aurelio García. "He had a falling out with these politicians and started to write a poison column in *Las Noticias,* bopping politicians and figures in the underworld and what have you. This is why he got it. He was not a bona fide reporter. He had never worked for a newspaper until he was kicked out of the PRI party here."

"Governor Esquivel Méndez, who succeeded Maldonado, was the one who brought Esprada Sastre to Baja," says Gorduno. "But something went wrong and he came to me for a job. He knew all the ins and outs of politics in Mexicali and started to write about it. I guess they thought he was going to put the finger on them for a lot of things that were supposedly secret. That's why he was killed."

It is estimated that the governor's cut on the vice *mordida* alone runs about ten million pesos a year. Considering the volume of activity, it seems a conservative enough figure. "The *mordida* goes to Mexicali," a brothel operator confided. "That's where the power is, where the governor resides. For example, a while back the Tijuana police closed the Chicago Club, and ten minutes later the state police opened it up. The *mordida* collected from whorehouses in Tijuana runs from eight to ten thousand dollars a week. One of the bagmen here for a long time was Jesús Váldez — he's known as *El Coyo*, which means 'little white rat.' He is a small fellow and very smart. He owns the El Barón, the Manhattan and Brooklyn bars, and the New York Hotel. He collected for the brother-in-law of the governor. The attorney general is the second man in the *mordida* setup. Last year *El Coyo* was replaced by Enrique Michaus, who was head of the state tourist bureau in Tijuana, but *Las Noticias* blasted him out of his job a few months ago [summer of 1967]. If a bar has rooms in back, they have to pay the *mordida*. If they don't, they charge the girl so much if she takes a customer to a hotel. The policeman at the door is always watching and he collects the *mordida*. There's plenty of this action and it involves a great deal of money."

"Enrique Michaus said he resigned from the tourist bureau to take a job with a private corporation but that was phony," says Gorduno. "What happened was that I started to knock him off. I said it was terrible to have somebody with a government job running vice here in Tijuana. So they ran him out. But they still have a representative of the cabdrivers' union in the tourist booth on Revolución, who fronts for all these pimps. From what I've heard, the governor's brother-in-law and the attorney general are involved directly in collecting the *mordida*. The attorney general is a close friend of Jesús Váldez, who runs the El Baron, a very rough place that's been closed many times for killing customers."

Former Tijuana mayor Gonzalo Nava blames the police for the situation. "A man comes up here from the interior," he says, "and figures, 'Well, I'm gonna be a cop for six months and see how much I can make before I go back to my home town.' He's not going to make the money honestly because the salary of policemen all over Mexico runs from eighty cents to three dollars a day. He's going to make it the only way he can — *mordida*. He's going to scare many people, a lot of them Americans. If he sees an American in a car, he'll come up and search it, maybe flash a little marijuana, and then say, 'I'll put you in jail or you give me five dollars now.' Well, they've given Tijuana a bad reputation. Some people say they split with the chief of police, or something like that. But it's not that. The situation, I believe, is that we don't have enough money yet to pay policemen a decent salary. So they have to make a little something for their pocket. But this is not just in Tijuana, this is everywhere in Mexico, especially in Mexico City."

"Everybody puts the bite on you," says Gorduno. "It works that way in everything. In other words, if you owe a tax bill, you go see the tax clerk and make a deal with him. You give him some money and he cuts the tax bill in half. Everybody is making money for himself at the expense of the government. The government loses ten times more money this way than if it paid people proper salaries. Civil servants are expected to make up the difference with graft. It's always been part of the system. Most of the money that comes into Tijuana goes to a few people here, a few people in Mexicali, and a few people in Mexico City. The cities are always in a state of bankruptcy. That's why we don't have streets and good water and sewage. We don't even have a library in Tijuana, a city of nearly three hundred thousand people. *Mordida* is the cancer of Mexico. It's a terrible thing and there doesn't seem to be any cure."

A Tijuana cabdriver told me that he paid 175 pesos ($14) a month *mordida*. "That's to protect me if I get a traffic or parking ticket," he said, "or if I get caught in a whorehouse or whatever may happen. It's like insurance. I don't have to worry about anything. Maybe we've got five thousand cabdrivers here and most of them pay it. That's a lot of money when you add it all up."

A young Chinese (a Mexican national) in Matamoros explained how he had fulfilled his military obligation. "I have my army service certificate," he said, "which everyone over eighteen has to have." (Military service is compulsory — every boy at eighteen must complete one year of training by attending army school on Sunday.) "The first Sunday I reported, I told the sergeant that I was going to school in Brownsville and that I needed my Sundays to study. He brought me to the captain, and he said, 'Well, how much can you pay?' The figure we arrived at was ten pesos a week, which I paid in a lump sum on graduation day. The general was there and there were some speeches and then I walked up and got my certificate. I had to pay customs two hundred pesos for a border-crossing card so I could attend school in Brownsville."

A bail bondsman from Austin, Texas, made a deal with the state police in Nuevo Laredo for the return of a narcotics smuggler who had jumped bail. For five hundred dollars, the state police agreed to return the fugitive. The exchange was to be made in the middle of the international bridge, but after the bondsman paid the money, the fugitive promised the police his brand-new Thunderbird if they would take him back into Mexico, which they promptly did, along with the bondsman's money.

Howard Walker, American consul in Piedras Negras, previously served in Brazil: "The *mordida* systems are quite similar in the two countries. I do think, however, that it's more pervasive here. The big problem in Mexico, and it's true to some extent in Brazil, is the terribly low salaries paid officials. It just will not support them. I can't remember what the mayor of Piedras Negras gets but I'm sure it's less than a hundred and fifty dollars a month. This is for the mayor of a municipality of about sixty thousand. In Brazil, for example, if I wanted to do business with the mayor, I didn't go to him directly. I went to a man who is called a *despachador,* who is literally an expediter. I paid him a certain amount of money for his services and whatever he thought he had to kick in along the way. You could go and sit in the mayor's office until you were blue in the face and not see anybody. All the offices, federal and otherwise, used *despachadores.* Even our consulate had one, and in many ways it was a tremendous convenience. I'm not kidding you. You didn't have to be bothered, it was all handled for you for a reasonable amount of money. It irked you on occasion, but at the same time, I mean there are advantages."

"The intrigue and treachery of our politics is too complex for an American mind to comprehend," a Mexican writer explained. "Your graft is simple by comparison. A Mexican politician is quite capable of a double double cross. Our federal government is the reverse of yours. Petty politicians are permitted to have petty rackets in your country, but this does not concern Washington, which would rather forget the whole damn thing. But in Mexico, there's never a road constructed, never even a minor deal transacted that the boys in Mexico City don't get their cut off the top. Here the cream always runs to the top. All PRI candidates for mayor, governor, senator, all elective offices, are selected by the power structure in Mexico City. All judges, prosecutors, high police officials, heads of economic and civic groups, everybody of any importance in the country, are passed upon by Mexico City. As you can see, this leaves little room for any kind of a dialogue between the people and the government. In the last election [1967], two PAN [*Partido de Acción Nacional*] candidates were elected mayor in Hermosillo [capital of Sonora] and Mérida [capital of Yucatán], but these cities are in real trouble now because the governors are PRI, not to mention Mexico City. In the same election, PRI candidates got ninety percent of the vote, winning all but one of the 178 contested seats in Congress. [The elections in Sonora and Yucatán were preceded by student riots.] It's traditional in Mexico for the parents to send the kids to do their fighting. In Hermosillo, for example, the thing that sparked the riot was the people's opposition to the PRI nominee for governor. Now PRI has been doing this for forty years, but suddenly the people are fed up. So out came the kids and for a while, until the army took over, there was some real fighting in the streets. An interesting sidelight is that the governor of Arizona sent arms and ammunition to the governor of Sonora, in violation of the Neutrality Act. So now we had Mexican students being shot down by American guns. The governor of Arizona defended his action on the grounds of the Good Neighbor Policy. That kind of a good neighbor Mexican people can do without.

"Well, you know, the power structure sticks together. Here in Mexico, the government is made up of a bunch of sycophants sucking up to the power structure, everybody flexing their *palanca,* fighting for a share of the budget and *mordida.* You see, *mordida* involves a lot more than vice and government contracts. It includes foreign investors who pay plenty for their concessions, and thousands of government employees who buy their jobs, particularly the kinds that offer a chance at *mordida.* Some jobs, like in customs, are bought in perpetuity — the father passes it on to the son, and it stays in the family like a legacy.

"Contrary to popular opinion, the president is not necessarily the man who runs Mexico. Have you heard the story of how Ruíz Cortines double-crossed everybody by threatening to go straight after he was elected president? He made a big speech about outlawing *mordida.* He was lucky he was not murdered.

"Another former president is greatly admired as the biggest thief in Mexican history. There's an old adage in my country that says, 'If a politician dies rich, he's a crook, and if he dies poor, he's stupid.' He was nothing but an impecunious lawyer before he went into politics, and now he's the richest man in Mexico. Besides having his finger in all kinds of American enterprises in Mexico, he owns property all over the world. I've heard it said that he has a ranch in every state in Mexico. At the end of his term, he left a whole bunch of half-constructed bridges and dams and office buildings, along with a false economy. Now, here's a man who really understands *mordida*. People admire him because he succeeded in a system that requires an incredible capacity for intrigue. *Mordida* is synonymous with politics. It's a way of life, a must if you want to succeed. And it's not only part of the government, but a part of the people, too. It will never change as long as we have a one-party system. Reforms are impossible when the people responsible are the bosses of the system."

In his book *The Mexicans*, Victor Alba takes *mordida* into the realm of meta-economics: "People say that corruption became common during Alemán's term in office and that no important business could function unless official elements had a share in it. It seems certain that many of the president's friends became wealthy, but as the proceeds of corruption were invested in the country, capital was created and Mexican capitalism grew strong enough to offset the damaging effect of the influx of foreign investment. . . . In truth, corruption can act as a policy of capitalization, provided that it does not last and is confined to small segments of society that invest their profits in the country, and provided that it does not lower the standard of living of the weakest economic groups. Such conditions were present in Alemán's time."

"There was this judge," says Marshall Hail, "whom I

knew, a very cultivated man, a violinist in the symphony, a man highly respected in Juárez. Then there was this American who saw he couldn't win a lawsuit through ordinary procedures. He paid the judge three thousand dollars to rule in his favor. As long as I've been here, I'm still amazed at the extensiveness of the *mordida* system. It seems to be part of a historical pattern. A recent mayor in Juárez was actually the bagman between Juárez and Mexico City at the time he was elected mayor. Even the Mexican press referred to him as the go-between in the vice operation which netted thirty thousand dollars a week. But the newspapers also collect *mordida,* usually in the form of a subsidy. When Governor Durán went into office in Chihuahua, he stopped the subsidy to José García Valsecca, who owns three dailies in Juárez and newspapers all over Mexico. Valsecca immediately started a campaign of vilification against the governor that went on until the subsidy was restored. Valsecca carries more bodyguards than the president, and well that he should, since he's probably the most feared and hated man in Mexico. Not only officials, but businessmen pay him *mordida.* But politics has become more stable in recent years. More conservative and more orderly. There was a time when no mayor or governor ever completed his term. Some lasted only a few weeks. There are probably more ex-mayors in Juárez than bartenders. I remember one mayor who was kidnaped by the governor's henchmen and taken clear down to Chihuahua, where he was told that if he wanted to survive, he'd best resign. We had one mayor who campaigned on a platform of getting rid of gangsters. As soon as he took office, a series of murders followed; nine gangsters were shot in the head and left at the entrance to the cemetery. No one was arrested and the rest of the gang either left town or fell into line, which meant that they had a new boss. In the Forties and Fifties, we had the Quevedo dynasty, which started with General Rodrigo Quevedo; they accumulated tremendous wealth. There were several generals in the family; and their sons were the kind who would go into a bar and say, 'I'm a Quevedo and when I drink, everybody drinks.' No one dared refuse; they were really *muy macho*. The way I understand Mexican politics, the president is the great white father and all power emanates down from him and his coterie of backers in the party. The governors are utterly dependent on him, and the mayors are utterly dependent on the governors. Congress is a rubber stamp. I don't know of one instance where it ever overrode the president. PRI today represents everyone who has money or expects to have."

One Juárez ex-mayor is Aureliano González Vargas, an attorney and politician of considerable expertise in border politics: "Government employees can't live on their wages. This makes it easy for them to bow to temptation. One of the bad features of Mexican fiscal policy is that state and municipal governments combined don't collect ten percent of what the federal government gets. Consequently, your local governments are in a state of perpetual economic chaos. The cities never have enough money and what happens is that you have to beg from the federal government. But to beg from the federal government, you need to go through the governor, or his feelings are going to be hurt. This creates a system of checks and balances, red tape that's put there to hold you in line. When you finally do succeed in cutting through a little *papeleo,* red tape, you feel like you've been given something magnanimously. This obligates you to the power structure. Everybody from the bottom up feels obligated to the leader directly above him, which is how power is accumulated. The way the system works, an aggressively intelligent man will not succeed in politics, which is still the fastest and surest way to wealth and power, because politicians are basically jealous and fearful. The father of a former governor who has been very successful politically, told me the secret of his son's success. He said, 'Don't ever let them know you have brains. Look at my son, he always acted stupid, he never knew anything, he was always asking questions and for advice. He got it free and he got it in huge quantities. He never frightened anyone, and look where he is today.' Well, today he's in Mexico City and doing very well, indeed.

"Mexico is a monolithic country with a powerful personality cult. You can do anything in Mexico except attack the president. That's taboo. Newspapers, radio, and television never attack the president. It's part of an unwritten law. The president is infallible, like the Pope, and above criticism. Why do we do that? We can take a minister and just tear him to shreds; call him all kinds of a

dumbbell, drunkard, pervert, and get away with it, because the laws of libel are just about impossible to en-
force. But if somebody gets in a corner and cusses out the
president, he'll be arrested, but when he arrives at the jail
somebody from the president's office will tell the police to
turn him loose. They lean over backward to create the
image of one that is all-powerful, all-gracious.

"Many of our ex-presidents are still powerful in PRI.
You know, the incumbent president selects his successor,
with advice, of course, from his backers. But he names
him, and many times remains a guiding force in the next
administration. But our country is maturing. Now our ex-
presidents draw life pensions, and if their wives outlive
them, they continue to receive the pensions. This came
about through a very painful experience years ago. In
order to support himself, Adolfo de la Huerta became a
voice teacher for Deanna Durbin in Hollywood. When
the government heard about it, they appointed him general supervisor of consulates in the United States and they
let him pick where he wanted to live, and he chose Los
Angeles. They said, 'All right, you've got so many thousands of dollars per month for salary, and we'll take care
of your office staff.' And he said, 'But I don't need an
office staff.' 'Oh, yes, you have to have an office and a staff;
just write your memoirs and don't teach singing anymore.' This shows one thing; maturity. The Revolution
has matured in the government and the government has
matured with the nation. We can't have these little
annoying things embarrass the country. It is now reaching

the stage where it can take care. We don't kill each other anymore. We just got over that. And we got over the one-lord idea, where a general was the commander of an army and where he went, the army went with him. We transfer them back and forth. We've got too many rich generals for them to risk a revolution.

"But we need far more changes. One of the biggest problems is that Mexico City is a suction center for all the money from the rest of the country. In recent years, some of the bigger cities like Guadalajara, Veracruz, and Puebla have raised hell and gotten some of their money back from Mexico City. But here on the border, we're the orphans. We're too far away. The vision in Mexico City is not all the way out here. Not yet. But there are signs that they are beginning to see that the border *is* Mexico — that it should be changed, that it should be beautified, that it should be helped, and that we are not all a bunch of thieves and crooked politicians. For years everything was so concentrated in Mexico City that it became a cumbersome giant. Industry, money, power, all of it was right there. Lately, the government has started to decentralize, to push things out to other cities. Pretty soon we're going to see real changes in the power structure itself. The old system is not capable of dealing with the complex problems of a developing nation, and that's what we are today. We're not an underdeveloped country any longer. Our gross national product is growing faster than that of the United States."

It is true that in the past decade the gross national

product has been growing an average of 6.5 percent a year (5.8 percent in the United States) and is exceeded only by that of West Germany and Japan. But it is equally true that the population growth rate is one of the highest in the world — 3.2 percent, or 1.4 million each year. The need for new jobs to match this growth is estimated at 500,000 a year, far more than the 180,000 presently created by industry, fifty percent of which is stimulated by government investment, while a large portion of the private investment is foreign.

The Revolution sacrificed more than a million lives for the promise of social and economic reform. Today, nearly sixty years later, the wealth of the nation remains concentrated in as comparatively few hands as ever. More than half the land is still controlled by wealthy ranchers (a new breed of mestizo and gringo *cacique*, leading citizen, has replaced the *gachupín*, Spaniard), and more than a million farm families earn an average income of less than a hundred dollars a year, in an economy where the price index on most basic commodities is higher than in the United States, and nearly doubles on luxury items. According to labor unions, half the country's fourteen million workers earn the bare official minimum wage (a dollar a day for farm labor in the interior to a top $3.00 in Baja California, which has the highest minimum wage in Mexico; it is a dollar fifty in Mexico City), and four million get even lower pay. Eleven million Mexicans cannot afford bread made from wheat and five million go barefoot. All of this in a nation of fifty million, and the population is expected to double in the next two decades.

Mexico is a country with limited natural resources, where two-thirds of the land is mountainous, where the rainfall is insufficient in the north and comes at the wrong time in the south, where millions of bitterly disappointed peasants have migrated to the cities in search of work or a handout. This problem is graphically illustrated in cities along the border.

"They come here by the thousands," says González Vargas, "and trap themselves. They have no place to go. What can they do? They can beg, borrow, steal or devote themselves to exploiting vice. What are we going to do about it? We can't deport Mexicans out to other parts of Mexico. What they didn't realize when they left their humble homes in the interior is that poverty in the interior is less demanding. Poverty here demands that they do something about it now if they hope to survive. We have these big, cold winds here and these people die like flies if they don't do something about proper shelter. In the interior, the weather is milder, and they can always pluck fruit that grows wild; they can take it easy. Sure, disease is prevalent down there. You have intestinal diseases, dysentery from fruits and vegetables, bad water, but here the diseases are scurvy, tuberculosis — can you imagine, children, ages nine and ten, die all the time from TB — malnutrition and some intestinal diseases in the summer. The problem is that border cities have grown much too fast. Juárez was about sixty thousand during the Second World War and now it's about five hundred thousand; El Paso was a hundred thousand and now it's three hundred thousand, but nearly fifty percent of that figure is Mexican-American."

"In Juárez," says Roberto Moya, "the rich and the poor make up about a hundred thousand, and then we have the really poor people and they make up the rest of the population. In Juárez, anyone making a hundred and fifty dollars a month is middle-class."

"Just imagine the way our city is growing," says Mayor López. "Tijuana is now three hundred thousand and these very humble people that you see on our streets just keep coming in here from the interior. Our state has the highest percentage of immigrated people in the country. Many of them want to go to the United States and they come here and stay with us while they try to get their permits. Others come here because of what they've heard about us, that we have the highest wage scale in the whole Mexican Republic. They sell their houses or their cows or whatever possessions they have, and come to Tijuana with their families, thinking they will find a job right away. Thousands of them stay but also a great percentage have to return. That causes big problems for us. We have in the city a budget to give return tickets to these people. Last year we bussed eight thousand back to the interior, but that is just a small number compared to the wetbacks the American Customs returned into the interior — they don't just drop them off at the border anymore, because right away they cross back again."

"Every day we are finding more ways to combat the

population problem," says González Vargas. "By next year we will have at least fifty American industries on this side of the border providing jobs for ten thousand of our people. This program, in a small way, will make up for the United States closing the door on the bracero in 1965, which left tens of thousands of farm workers stranded in border cities."

Optimism for the Frontier Industrialization program runs high in border cities where unemployment and underemployment ranges from sixty percent in Tijuana to eighty percent in Matamoros. How massive the program will be has yet to be determined. American labor officials are already expressing concern over the long-range effect of this apparently endless pool of cheap labor on their own organizations.

By January 1, 1968, some two years after the Mexican Government initiated the program, thirty-four American companies had established plants in half a dozen cities, employing some five thousand persons, and representing a total investment of about eight million dollars. Besides the availability of cheap labor, the Mexican inducement includes tax and tariff privileges provided the manufactured product is shipped back to the United States.

William Harper, a member of the El Paso Chamber of Commerce, has been working on the program with American investors since its inception. "One of the most frustrating aspects," he says, "is the need for a contact in Mexico City. Each plant is a result of individual negotiations. There is no clear, hard or fast set of rules. A great deal of it is ad-libbed by the wrong people. Picking the right contact among a long list of alleged cousins claiming to represent the one and only right contact is the big problem. The point is that nothing moves until you do find the right contact, because approval from Mexico City is imperative. But even after this has been accomplished, there are other pitfalls which I'd rather not go into at the moment. Suffice it to say that Mexico does everything within its power to protect its own industrial growth. For example, if a Mexican manufacturer starts making light bulbs, whatever their quality, the government promptly slaps restrictions on their importation. This means that American plants must forthwith use Mexican light bulbs. This is the reason Mercedes Benz moved out of Mexico — a Mexican company began manufacturing engine blocks and Mercedes was obliged to take them, which they flatly refused. And I can't say I blame them. How can you maintain the integrity of your product if you are forced into this sort of compromise?"

"All of these concessions," says Roberta Ridgely, a seasoned reporter of the Tijuana scene, "have been on the books a long time, but nobody had done much talking about border industries until the Watts riots. Then the idea of all this tractable cheap labor began to look pretty good to certain people in Los Angeles. I think it's a good idea for a small operation, but if it got big it would get nothing but trouble."

"The only industries that should come in here are those that are doomed because of competition from foreign markets like Japan and Hong Kong," says Mayor López. "Now if they keep the highly skilled workers over there and have the rough part of the work down here with our cheap labor, both of them in combination, they will get a better product than the foreign market and at a good competitive price. It means a very small capital investment for the Americans. Mostly they rent buildings and move in their machines, so the risk is minimal. Many are afraid of our unions because they are very strong, but it's not a question of their strength that's important. If you make a profit, you have to renew the union contract every two years, and then they will ask for an increase in wages."

"My impression of unions," says Marshall Hail, "is that they are just an arm of the government. Regardless of how radical they may appear, or how loaded the laws are in their favor, they never seem to accomplish very much as far as improving the standard of living of their members. To call a strike, all they have to do is plant a red and black flag in front of your business, and you are closed. You can't even cross your own property line. The merits of the case have little to do with the settlement of it. If the strike reaches an impasse, it eventually will work its way to the top and be settled on a political basis. This is what is called a red union, an independent union aligned with PRI. There's another type, company sponsored, called white unions, and controlled by large employers who tend to be paternalistic. They provide recreation facilities, free medical benefits, and quite often beans and rice at cost. In return, the workers don't demand too much in money wages. The situation is analogous to our labor movement in the early 1900's before the AFL–CIO gained power."

Lindsey Rhodes is a "proud" Texan by way of Louisiana and Los Angeles, and a public relations man by way of engineering school. He is middle-height, middle-weight and middle-aged. He is well groomed, well fed (his bland, round, smooth face is surprisingly youthful), and well opinionated on a multitude of subjects. His tightly curled hair is tightly cropped, and his tightly woven vocabulary is delivered in tightly packed spurts. In Brownsville, his adopted home, he is the Chamber of Commerce's expert on the Frontier Industrialization program.

Seated before a tape recorder in his office, his demeanor is the quintessence of the P.R. syndrome. He rubs his hands, he leans confidently toward the mike, he smiles sincerely, and underneath it all, he vibrates with information that must somehow be translated into a soft sell. "Oh, yes," he says, "we are absolutely a hundred percent behind this border program. Never forget for a moment that Mexico is the number one consumer of the U.S. Our philosophy reflects this fact. We say, whatever is good for Mexico is good for the U.S. and vice versa. We say, forget the Orient if you are oriented toward a high labor content. We say, if your labor content is twenty percent or above, come to Mexico if you wish to compete in the world market. We say, for every dollar created by payroll in Matamoros and every dollar spent, five additional are created — five, eight, or nine, whatever the factor is. For every hundred industrial jobs, a hundred and seventy-five are generated — this is an industrial fact. That's why it's so important to convince American industry to come to the border instead of going to the Orient, which does the United States no damn good. Here they can utilize the high labor content and get control of the time dimension. We say, consider the total economics of everything involved. Then come to the border.

"We don't say it's perfect. There are minor problems yet to be ironed out. But Mexico itself has been real stable, the peso has been stable over a long period, and the government is strong and stable. The dangers, primarily, are in the preliminary negotiations. You see, when you move into Mexico, you're vulnerable to an atmosphere in which everyone says I'm the one, I've got the channels, my uncle has got this, I know this guy in Mexico City, and all this and that and the other. But there are very definitely the right people, as there are also very definitely the wrong people. Unfortunately, Mexican law tends to be a bit nebulous. If it were simple, we could just pick up documents and know. That would do away with lawyers. So let's face it. Legislation anywhere in the world is made for one reason, and that's to create the services of people to facilitate and service you to that point. It's what makes the world go round. It's nebulous and it's staying nebulous for a reason.

"Here's what we say to prospective investors. We say, do a complete research analysis and a feasibility report in depth. Start with U.S. Customs to determine the duties

involved and then take a long look into the local environ-
ment — political, economic and social. Determine the type
of labor content available. Here in Matamoros we are
basically oriented to agriculture. The cotton business was
producing a half-million bales and now it's down to fifteen thousand. So we have nothing but labor here. Juárez,
on the other hand, is a high economic pulsating community relative to El Paso — it has economics that are
pressure pushed at a higher level than we have. Tijuana
has the highest labor economics of the entire border —
three dollars a day. Wages get progressively lower as you
approach the Caribbean, with Matamoros the lowest at
two dollars and eight cents. The one factor that is constant on the entire border is surplus labor, from forty to
eighty percent labor availability. These figures include
people who live by their wits, or perform service-oriented
functions like tourism.

"Another factor we say you must take into consideration is that Mexico does not possess a high broad-based
literacy level. Subordinate people in responsible positions
are not usually as capable in handling basic functions. The
thing you have to remember when you move into Mexico
is that you have to think Mexican. The channels of
communication from the top to the bottom are slow;
there is a lot of lag and loss. That's why we fully subscribe
to their one-party system of government. It's the only way
they can maintain stability and effect change. Just look at
France, parties upon parties; they'll never have stability.
De Gaulle was the only one keeping them together and

this guy was long past his bedtime even when he went in this last time. Mexico effects change within a system, a fixed system of organization. They don't have disruptions with every election, with a new party wasting years trying to get acclimated. All we say is that if you have to live down here on the border, you have to become embedded within the fabric of understanding.

"We give American business the best advice we are capable of giving them. We hand carry each one. We're not saying, do it exactly as we say. We say, this is a manner of procedure which you can follow. Now look at alternate ways and means of doing it and plug it into your automated equipment and see how it comes out.

"As for myself, I was born and reared in Louisiana, but I spent twenty years in Los Angeles and I claim that as my home. But now I'm a Texan by desire, by choice. I'm a converted Texan, and, as such, I feel that I might tend to be more objective than one who is native-born. Because in my work I have to follow facts. And there's the very fact that in 1940 when I arrived in Los Angeles it was two million and when I left in 1960 it was seven and a half million, and I had the benefit of a five and a half million growth. I'd say this was an experience that very few people have the opportunity to enjoy in a lifetime. And I hope I can contribute through the benefit of this observation to the growth of this area. Life is what you make of it, and home has always been anywhere I hang my hat, because I love people. I think that people who have this feeling are preoccupied with certain things that's within

the makeup of their own fiber. Some of the Mexican
people I've met here are some of the finest I've enjoyed.
And the longer I stay here, the more in love with Mexico I
become. I mean this most sincerely."

Later, on a guided tour of Brownsville and Matamoros,
with the tape recorder packed away, he launches into a
free-associative monologue. "I tell you, this lower Rio
Grande valley area is unique, really rare in its cohesive-
ness. The valley pulls together, on both sides of the river.
Nearly a million people in terms of sixty, seventy miles,
and that's one megalopolis. And let me tell you something very special, the Negro problem here is less than one-
half of one percent. Well, I've been through that monkey
race in Los Angeles and Louisiana, and I've had it; I mean
right up to here. . . . Look at this park, see the *resaca*,
they make this city a garden spot. This is God's country.
. . . Oh, sure, we have problems. Unions are against us.
But we know what kind of hypocrites those guys are. Sure,
they wave flags against the program, trying all the time to
figure ways of getting in on it themselves. . . . Now, I
won't let you write about this, but in my opinion the two
most malignant forces in American society are unions and
newspapers. The press never reports anything accurately.
And, of course, you can understand why when you see the
kind of people you have working for the press. I don't
hold anything against book writers like yourself, but what
can you expect from a business that pays such low salaries.
All they get is people without talent, drunks mostly, who
are making up things to impress their boss. . . . Look

around, we're in the main shopping district of Brownsville. Oh, what fantastic business stores do. One hundred and thirty thousand Mexicans right across the bridge
and most of them shop here. Why, you could sell garbage
here and they'd come and just grab it; you know, they'd
fight for it. You really, honestly could sell garbage. That's
how hungry these Mexicans are for American goods. . . .
Well, now we're in Mexico. Oh, my goodness, look at all
these bodies, look at them; two dollars and eight cents a
day and you can take your pick. Look at these units, look
at them, isn't it great. Look anywhere, in any direction;
they're everywhere. Oh, I love these people. We could
work here. I tell you it makes your head spin. Such warm-
hearted people. . . . Want some liquor while we're
down here? Must lock the car. I hope the wheels are still
on when we get back. . . . You can buy any brand American cigarettes for a dollar-fifty a carton. Don't worry about
U.S. Customs. We've got them working with us and
nobody really gets excited about these things. It makes
the wheels turn — it makes progress, and business. Smuggling? Now, that's your term. You're looking for a fine
law. Wouldn't it be pitiful if we lived exactly to law. We
have too many rules and regulations that govern us right
now. It would probably put us in our death grave if we
looked at all of them."

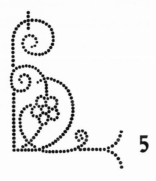

5

El Contrabando

Smuggling has long been a way of life on the border, from Mexican children peddling untaxed American cigarettes on international bridges to the *contrabandista* who hauls an enormous generator under the bridge because *"señor,* it is *muy grande* to pass over it."

It would be challenging, indeed, to conjure up an item that could not be smuggled in either direction if the price were right. Surprisingly, most of the smuggling (except for narcotics) is going south — everything, in fact, from guns to lard.

Literally thousands of *fayuqueros* (little smugglers) do a brisk business in contraband groceries, used clothing, cigarette lighters, ballpoint pens, and sundry small items

— about ninety percent of all American merchandise either is prohibited or requires a special import permit, and duties imposed on the remaining ten percent usually equal one hundred percent of the value.

"We are still living in the old days of the high tariff wall," says González Vargas. "Besides making everything so much more expensive, it encourages smuggling, not only on the border but in the interior. You pay duty on one item and bring in nine with the connivance of customs. People in Juárez spend three million pesos a day in El Paso on such ridiculous things as milk and foodstuff. Eggs, of all things, when El Paso doesn't have enough chickens and has to import them from Los Angeles. They buy bread that's three and four days old, and milk at the supermarkets that's five days old — it comes on trucks all the way from Georgia. Our Juárez milk, which is perfectly good, has to be sold in Sinaloa. This foolishness is very bad on our economy."

Historically, Mexican bordertowns have been dependent on their American counterparts for most of the necessities and all of the luxuries of life. Until recent times, there was no manufacturing and little food processing anywhere on the Mexican side. Many of the towns were isolated from the interior by vast mountainous regions and poor, if any, transportation — the first paved road between Mexico City and Tijuana was not completed until 1957, and telephone connection between the two cities is still by radio. As a consequence, shopping *al otro lado* long ago developed into a powerful habit for countless thousands of Mexicans who still prefer foreign goods, believing they are better and cheaper.

Mexican Customs collectors could not agree more with their *compadres* — it involves millions in *mordida*. "The border is so profitable," says a consular official, "that Mexican Customs rotates its officers to give them all a chance at it."

The beauty of the system, from this point of view, is that only a few of the contraband items have been publicly identified. The fabled "list" of prohibited American goods is a mystery even to U.S. Customs. In a two-hour interview which I had with the head of Mexican Customs in Mexicali (attended by five interpreters), fewer than a dozen items were reluctantly named, and requests for the official list were met with shrugs and grunts, leaving the impression that even their own officers were working in the dark and quite happy about it — who could challenge them as they ad-libbed the list?

The stated purpose of the list is to protect Mexican industries, but there are those who look upon smuggling as an industry in itself. "Let's not kid ourselves," says a U.S. Customs official, who admits to having turned cynical after "too many years" on the border, "the list is geared to the *mordida* system. They can't be that stupid; they know perfectly well that a lot of these items are not available in Mexico, and putting them on the list has nothing to do with promoting their industry. It promotes smuggling and *mordida,* and don't think it's not planned that way. It's a system that collects by every possible means available. The problem is, they can't control it, isolate it to certain items and areas. Every time a Mexican crosses to the U.S. and buys a television set or refrigerator, washing machine or suit, anything that's manufactured in Mexico, and smuggles it in, he's damaging the country's economy in countless ways — employment, taxes, buying power, trade balance, and so forth. In my opinion, *mordida*, this government by personal fortune, is devouring the country and is one of the main reasons for the poverty and misery that goes on year after year without change."

The *fayuquero* is not concerned with his country's economy. He has enough trouble worrying about his own. Early in the morning he drives his stripped-down jalopy across the boundary and loads up with contraband groceries, his small bankroll being the only talent that separates him from the multitudes who beg or hustle to survive through each day. Later, after he has bribed a customs inspector (for roughly ten percent of the wholesale value of his cargo) to look the other way, he will hawk his wares on the streets at a profit of upward of fifty percent. Many *fayuqueros* shop for restaurants and markets in their towns. Others are buyers for curio and variety stores in need of countless small items popular with tourists and available in the United States at much lower prices.

Meanwhile, tens of thousands of men and women with *micas* (border-crossing permits) will make their daily pilgrimage to the gringo supermarket, carrying back barely enough food to last the day — a hard fact of life in homes without refrigeration, some shop for each meal. The *mordida* — after the inspector has peeked into each parcel — will run a few centavos, unless lard is found. Although seldom available in Mexican bordertowns, lard appears to be *número uno* on the list. Others will bring in used clothing, which was recently identified as definitely on the list, and here the bite will be bigger. "I know you won't believe this," one official told me, "but I've seen Mexican Customs inspectors wearing change makers on their belts. You want to hear some wild jingling sounds, just bump into any one of these guys coming off duty after the six o'clock rush. Their pants pockets hang down to their kneecaps — no Continental cut there, man."

Mexico's National Bank of Foreign Trade places the annual loss of revenues from uncollected duties at a quarter-billion dollars, an amount about equal to what is presently being collected from all goods legally entering the country. This would indicate that duties are being collected on at least fifty percent of all imports, but this is far too optimistic, since most of the border trade is conducted in American currency. Americans spend dollars in borderland towns, which are promptly returned by Mexicans. In Juárez, for example, Mexican records indicate imports valued at only ten million dollars a year, whereas the El Paso Chamber of Commerce estimates that Mexicans buy nearly fifty million dollars of retail goods each year. A U.S. federal commission estimated that Mexicans spent eighty million dollars in San Diego in 1967. And these figures would not include contraband in the purview of the *contrabandista:* untaxed liquor and cigarettes from export stores, industrial and farm machinery, large appliances, construction material, guns and ammunition.

Nor would the above figure include the thousands of automobiles driven with American registrations in border cities — twenty-eight thousand in Juárez alone. (Car thieves enjoy a superlative business. Once a stolen car crosses the line, it is unlikely the owner will ever see it in one piece again — the practice is to strip it for parts as rapidly as humanly possible.) The border is the only place a Mexican may indulge his whim for a high-status car; fancy, imported cars are not permitted in the interior — nothing over six cylinders. Nine of the twelve models sold in Mexico are made in Mexico by Ford, General Motors, Chrysler and American Motors, and retail at about double the price similar models sell for in the United States. The other three are Volkswagen, Renault and Datsun. The biggest models available are the Ford Galaxie, Dodge Coronet and Chevrolet Impala. The Cadillac, Lincoln or Rolls Royce are strictly illegal.

"But there are tricks to all trades," says González Vargas. "You do see Mexicans driving big cars in the interior. They get somebody who has a U.S. residence and have it put in their name. Every six months, he drives to the border and has the permit renewed. Or they find somebody in the diplomatic corps, some poor vice-consul, who is allowed to sell his car after he's had it one year."

One explanation behind this restriction (that is, the

political psychology) is the government's fear of flaunting wealth in a country where the rich are so few and so imposingly rich, and the poor are so very, very many and so abjectly poor.

Compared to the *fayuquero*, the *contrabandista* is an entrepreneur of considerable means and talent — and, of course, connections. He supplies not only the necessities, but the luxuries of life as well: water heaters, color television sets, bathroom fixtures, tape recorders, refrigerators, irons — anything anybody can afford.

A consular official in Monterrey looks upon the *contrabandista* as an impetus to the economy: "Let's be realistic for a moment. Let's say you have a factory here in Mexico and you need a lathe that sells for fifty thousand dollars in the States. A similar lathe is available here in Mexico for a hundred thousand but delivery may take six months to a year. What are you going to do? Close down operation and wait so that you can pay twice as much for something which in all probability is inferior? Hell, no. You'll get a *contrabandista* and he'll load the American lathe on a truck and bring it across. He may spend a few thousand in the right places, but you'll be back in business, *pronto*. To me, this keeps the economy moving. It may be corruption in one sense, but it keeps the people in your factory working. Even if the lathe were not available in Mexico, getting the necessary import permit from Mexico City could take a year and the duties would run a hundred percent. They just don't give a businessman any alternative."

The *contrabandista*'s loyalty is not legendary. The double-cross is a ploy of his trade. He lives in a world where possession is ten-tenths of the law. "I bought a nice refrigerator in San Diego for three hundred dollars," a Tijuana businessman explained, "and made a deal with a smuggler to bring it in for fifty dollars. I waited a few days for delivery and then went down to Guadalajara on business. The first night I was gone, my wife called to say that the smuggler and refrigerator had arrived, accompanied by a customs inspector. The bite was two hundred dollars or no refrigerator — still it was cheaper than if I had bought it here in Mexico."

As a result of import restrictions, monopolies abound in Mexico. For example, in the states of Chihuahua and Baja, there is only one manufacturer of cement. In Juárez, cement is imported from the city of Chihuahua, 240 miles away, at a cost of a dollar sixty a bag; and contractors claim it is about two-thirds the potency of cement available in El Paso at one dollar a bag. In Baja, the monopoly is held by General Clark Flores in Enseñada, and the discrepancies in quality and price are similar to those in Juárez. What this means to construction costs, public or private, is plainly obvious. What it means to the *contra-bandista* is another market.

There are no limits to the variety of merchandise being smuggled into Mexico. Three *contrabandistas* specialized in condemned and contaminated meat, which they purchased from federally uninspected meat plants in Hobbs and Clovis, New Mexico, and sold to restaurants and meat markets in Juárez. On the day they were apprehended by U.S. Customs, they had filed declaration forms listing their cargo as beef heads, pork skins, beef livers and dog meat valued at $174. But invoices in their possession indicated the total value at $543 — four complete beef carcasses had not been declared. Investigation disclosed they had been making weekly trips for three years — the number of people killed in this period by tainted meats was anybody's guess.

Guns and ammunition is big business in Latin American countries. Otherwise, *señor*, how could one enjoy the fruits of a revolution? The biggest gun-running case ever cracked by U.S. Customs on the border took place in El Paso. The investigation, which dragged for eleven years, began in 1954, when agents arrested an American soldier attempting to smuggle rifles into Mexico. He confessed, implicating Pete Muñoz, a resident of Juárez and the owner of an El Paso hardware store. But the case against Muñoz was too circumstantial to pursue in the courts. Four years later, Mexican police at an interior checkpoint caught a smuggler with a truckload of arms, and again a shaky circumstantial trail led to Muñoz's hardware store. Then in 1964, U.S. Customs received an anonymous letter stating that a Mexican posing as a cattle buyer was a gun-runner. Upon his arrest, he too implicated Muñoz. The hardware store was finally placed under surveillance. An agent, who tailed a customer for a week, tells what happened next: "This guy was so sure of himself that he crossed into Mexico a half-dozen times with twenty-seven rifles hidden under the seats of his car and ammo in the door panels. Once he went over just for a haircut, that's how sophisticated he was. Well, we busted him and secured a search warrant for the hardware store, but by the time we arrived, Muñoz had skipped back to Juárez. We checked invoices and found serial numbers to match the twenty-seven rifles we'd confiscated. But it wasn't until we started going through Muñoz's records that we really knew the size of the operation. We found stacks of correspondence to his Mexican customers, advising them to get their full orders in immediately so that he would not have to piecemeal it down, at greater cost, but could load it on tractor-trailers where he could conceal eighty thousand dollars worth of merchandise each trip. The store turned out to be an arsenal, with enough equipment to arm every man, woman and child in El Paso. His inventory included two million rounds of .22 ammo and a bunch of .308 Army ammo that was still in the process of being distributed to continental units. We had a good case, but no luck in extraditing Muñoz, who now lives in a big house in Juárez, kitty-corner from the American Consulate on Sixteenth of December Street — a few months later he was even invited to the home of an American vice-consul for Thanksgiving dinner. Mexican officials have since confiscated two loads of U.S. Army automatic rifles, and the word is that it cost Muñoz fifty thousand dollars to buy his way out. So he's still in business, which means he's getting stuff across the line."

Another recent El Paso smuggling case involved a ring that boasted it could deliver any type of weaponry, in-

cluding fighter planes, tanks and submarines. The ring
was composed of a restaurateur, a stockbroker, a customs broker, an airplane pilot, and two college students.
Their first mistake was to plot openly in a café frequented
by federal agents and newsmen. Their second (and final)
mistake was to trust a "buyer" in Mexico and a "supplier"
in California (they offered a twenty-million-dollar order)
who turned out to be undercover agents for U.S. law enforcement agencies.

For years, the term "rum run" has referred to gringos
hauling rum and tequila to the American side in vast
quantities, at prices that made it worthwhile. Until 1965,
when U.S. federal restrictions on liquor imports went into
effect, residents from Brownsville to Yuma (Californians,
due to a strong liquor lobby, were excluded) were allowed
to bring in one gallon per month for every member of the
family, children included. The new law reduced it to one
quart and none for children. Yet even in its heyday (except during Prohibition), the "rum run" coming out of
Mexico was never as great as the one going into it.

The *contrabandista* has a ready-made, tax-free source of
supply at U.S. export stores along the entire border. Here
cigarettes and liquor from all over the world are available
at discounts of up to sixty percent. If he were to bring it
into Mexico legally, the duties and taxes would run one
hundred percent of the value.

"The way I feel as an American citizen and a customs
officer is that we ought not to help Mexicans smuggle into

Mexico. I don't give a damn whether their officials are crooked or not. We should not be part of any smuggling ventures into Mexico. Check on the Mexican side and you'll find that liquor in bars is purchased at export stores on the American side. I don't think we're acting in good faith, because our customs official stands right there by the smuggler's car and watches him hide the liquor. Another thing is that our customs official does not go up to the border with the load as he should, but stays back so that the Mexican inspectors can't see that here comes the export man with a load of liquor. He actually hides behind a corner so they can't see him. Is this showing good faith? What do I care what gets through Mexican Customs as long as it is bona fide on our part? If their officials want to take a bribe, fine — it's none of my business. But, hell, this customs official will even supervise it into a plane. He will watch them load up a plane with liquor — and this all happens within the United States — and supposedly observes it being exported to a foreign destination. At other times, the liquor is taken out into the country and loaded into trucks, and the customs official follows the load back to the border and watches it exported. I don't think our government sanctions this. Every once in a while the Mexicans stand up and say, 'You know this stuff is being smuggled; why don't you stop it?' And our officials say, 'Oh, it's all legal as far as our laws are concerned.' But it's not legal. We are one of the devious parties involved; we are co-conspirators. I've been told by certain people to stay away from this or I'll get my head chewed off by some political highups. I've been told this many times by many people. Well, maybe, but if enough of us raise hell, Washington will have to put a stop to it. The *mordida* system is so common here on the border that our own government goes along with it. Nobody gets upset over it. It's just the system — this is the way it is. Sometimes a Mexican official will open up and kind of brag about the *mordida* he collects. Then he'll say, 'Look, can I afford to be honest?' And the gringo, whose salary is ten times that of the Mexican, will say, 'Of course, you can be honest.' But look at the situation. This man's boss is in on it and the men working above and below him are in on it. The businessman, by offering the payoff, is in on it. The politician, by demanding a cut, is in on it. How long can he be honest before he's kicked out? The system cannot stand an honest man. If you want to know how much money there is in *mordida*, go look at the home of the former head of customs in Mexicali. He's retired and lives in the most fabulous house in town. He's even got a bomb shelter stocked with a year's provisions."

In Texas, from Del Rio, south of the Big Bend country, to Brownsville, on the Gulf of Mexico, United States Customs regulations are the most relaxed on the border. Here Texans or tourists cross into Mexico and purchase not only Mexican liquor but also untaxed (smuggled) export-store liquor at fantastic savings and bring it back across merely by paying a nominal state tax — the inspector will automatically stamp the top of the bottle without opening the paper sack. The one-quart-per-month stipulation of Mexican liquor means one quart per trip. I made four trips within an hour in Brownsville, bringing one bottle each time to the same inspector, who stamped it with a smile and a nod of recognition for my easily identifiable Italian sportscar. (In Nogales, along the Arizona border, inspectors inquire each time as to the date of the last purchase.) Cartons of American cigarettes, any brand, sell at prices ranging from two dollars in Acuña to a dollar fifty in Matamoros — and no questions asked. I came through customs and pointed to five cartons uncovered in the front seat and was waved on without a question.

A Californian hoping to bring in liquor or cigarettes at ports in his state will have to devise unique smuggling techniques. "There are ways," says an inspector. "There are some pretty good pros in this business, but the guy you really have to watch out for is the friendly one. He gets established real fast. He may live in California or in Mexico, and he will cross the line twenty times a day for two or three weeks, until he gets to know everybody on a first-name basis. He won't be bringing zilch the first two weeks or so, but brother when he is established and everybody is on a first-name basis — 'Hi, Joe,' and they wave him on down the road — this is the guy that's going to put a hook into you. We caught a Mexican recently, a lieutenant colonel, who knew everybody on the line, and when we finally busted him, we found that he was bringing in booze by the caseload to friends in San Diego, including a couple of bank vice-presidents and an inspector in the Highway Patrol."

On the flip side of the smuggling record, the most popular items coming into the United States (besides the steady flow of narcotics) include candelilla wax, mercury, silver, watch movements, jewelry, pre-Columbian artifacts, diamonds, gold bullion and coins, pornographic movies, dirty books and pictures, parrots and parakeets, cattle, and people. Compared to people, usually called "wetbacks," the other traffic is comparatively light.

For example, there is little point in smuggling gold into the United States when Asian markets will pay extravagant prices for any quantity. Consequently, the glitter of gold on the border is mostly in the eye of the swindler. The "Yaqui brick" has long been his most persuasive commodity. The idea is to interest a rich prospect in the fables of Indian chiefs who stockpiled gold bullion in hidden temples. "It's not unusual for them to talk in terms of a million ounces of gold," says Charles Cameron, customs agent in charge in Nogales. "The way they paint the picture, there's practically no danger in it. So the mark leaves his home and comes down to Nogales or some other bordertown, and first thing he knows, he's meeting all kinds of mysterious people, who shuttle him from town to town — Tucson, Las Vegas, Hermosillo, Chihuahua. Phone calls come in at all hours of day and night, telegrams fly all over the place; and if necessary, he is taken out to an abandoned mine in the hills, and there he sees Yaqui Indians armed with rifles and *bandoleras*, the whole bit, and is told they are guarding the treasure. He finally winds up in a crummy room in some small Mexican town and is there presented with brass-plated lead bricks and told to drill a sample and to leave his seal on the bricks. They give him an envelope to hold the filings, and suddenly there's a knock at the door and everybody gets very excited. In the confusion, the envelopes are switched, and the mark takes real gold filings back to the States for assay. We had two fellows from New York not too long ago who put down fifty-two thousand dollars on bricks that held their seal, and when we told them it was lead, they wouldn't believe us. They thought we were trying to steal their gold — after all, their seal was there and the assay had certified it was gold."

This confidence game is also played with Canadian bullion, supposedly hijacked from government shipments and smuggled into Mexico. The quoted price is thirty-two dollars an ounce, and if the prospect looks like a pretty good thief, they offer to help him move it to Hong Kong, where the market price is forty dollars and up an ounce. "The routines are similar," says Cameron. "With Canadian gold, it usually winds up in a hotel room on this side of the line, with the mark's money stacked nicely in a briefcase, ready for the transfer, when suddenly the phone rings, and the con man cries out, 'My God, the feds are coming; so-and-so has been arrested; let's get out of here fast.' The con man grabs the briefcase and his accomplice, usually the original contact, pushes the mark out the door. Well, this is pretty exciting stuff, and once out in the street, the contact, who's shaking with fear, will lead the mark to a new hotel, while the con man takes off with the money. Once in the room, the contact will give his Academy Award performance, crying, 'Oh, my God, I'm gonna get arrested; we're going to the penitentiary, I just know it. Well, I'm getting out of it. I'm not taking any more risks.' He'll bemoan the fact he's out several thousand dollars for expenses, 'but I'm not going to prison for a few thousand bucks.' He'll order the mark to stay in the room while he tries to locate the boss, who will call the mark with new instructions for delivery of the gold. After he leaves, the mark sits there and stares at the walls until it finally dawns on him that he's been had. Chances are he'll pack up and go home — and forget it. The problem is that he's also a thief, usually a respected businessman or doctor, someone who has money Uncle Sam doesn't know anything about. The last thing he wants is for anybody to know that he was down in Mexico trying to buy gold. It would be impossible to guess how many people get caught in this racket, but we hear about it every month. There's always somebody calling up to tell us about some smuggler down in Mexico who has thousands of ounces of gold that he's trying to sell. We work it long enough to find the con game."

It may have all the cornball appeal of a television melodrama, but even more outlandish ploys succeed regularly on the border. Take the Interpol caper known as "The Swindle of Double Emission of Bank Notes." It was very popular in 1964. It began with businessmen in Guadalajara and El Paso receiving authentic Banco de México notes in the amounts of five, ten and twenty dollars. They were informed that the bank notes were samples of merchandise being manufactured in a printing shop in the United States with authentic paper and ink, and that they were available at a very reasonable price. If the customer indicated the least interest, he was presented with a box of bicolored pencils and asked to break them in half — *caramba*, inside each pencil was a neatly rolled bank note. Now convinced of a fabulous profit, the customer was ready to do business. After having agreed on a price, the exchange was made in a public place — a small packet of money for a large box of pencils. Later, in the privacy of his room, the customer discovered, as in the gold caper, that there is a lot of lead in Mexico.

Two words, exploitation and wetback, are synonymous on the border. For more years than most people care to remember, the Mexican migrant worker has been the secret weapon of the gringo farmer, from the "salad bowl" south of San Diego to the "fruit bowl" of the lower Rio Grande valley.

The literature of exploitation is shocking beyond credibility, and yet it is true — all the injustice and suffering and bestiality of indentured labor, all the avarice and cruelty and rationalization of a system built on the exigency of profit.

Unlike the bracero, who enjoyed the illusion of legality, the wetback is an outlaw in search of an exploiter. He becomes an economic unit the moment desperation drives him toward *Los Estados Unidos*. His first contact will be the *contrabandista*, who just happens to have the right spot all picked out for him. For his troubles, depending on his arrangement with the gringo farmer or manufacturer, the *contrabandista* will collect anywhere from a hundred to three hundred dollars a head from his sponsor and as much from the wetback as he can squeeze — and chances are the gringo will later deduct his expense from the wetback's wages.

Not all *contrabandistas* have connections in the United States. Some will merely transport the wetback over the line; others will take him a few hundred miles to large cities like Los Angeles, Tucson or San Antonio and dump him there to shift for himself, a stranger without money, papers, or language.

And not all *contrabandistas* are Mexicans. There is the legendary gringo (a fugitive from the pages of *To Have and Have Not*) known as El Alemán, who haunts the waters between Enseñada and San Diego in his *El Espectro*. El Alemán, one of the few to extend credit, will transport wetbacks to beaches along Mission Bay in San Diego where other gringos will drive them to Los Angeles, or sometimes to customers as far north as Oregon and Washington.

Known in the old days as "wire jumpers," wetbacks today use all means of transportation, from walking to flying. They have been hidden under tons of manure, pressed into empty gasoline and vinegar tankers, secreted among furniture in U-Haul trailers, and jammed into automobile trunks. Some undoubtedly have come in by submarine, and others will one day do it in a rocket. Along the shallow Rio Grande, wading guides hire out to women and children so they won't step into holes and drown. In the early Forties, they would gather by the thousands on their side of the invisible line, across from Arizona and California, and on signal would come charging over, barreling through the meager forces of the Border Patrol. Thousands made it across fields and mountains to large cities and war-plant jobs, and like other minorities before them, they ended up in the American ghetto.

Every year U.S. Immigration returns thousands of wetbacks to their homeland — 146,000 in 1968. Many have made the round trip often. One wetback, with a compulsive fondness for El Paso, was flown deep into the interior of Mexico fifty-seven times. He became celebrated in the El Paso press as the "Champion Wetback."

The bracero was outlawed in 1965, but the Green Card program, which allows a worker to reside in Mexico and work in the United States, has been in effect forty years. In 1968, the Select Commission on Western Hemisphere Immigration estimated the number of Green Card workers at forty thousand, which may or may not be close. No one seems to know for sure. Green Card workers form about eighty percent of the seven thousand farm workers of the Imperial Valley across from Mexicali and nearly ninety percent of the twenty thousand garment workers in El Paso. Another ten thousand work at various service jobs in San Diego, and countless thousands toil in the Rio Grande valley, preferring gringo wages even if they are below standards for American workers. A Green Card holder residing in the United States has the status of *emigrado* and may become a citizen after five years.

Perhaps as many as a million Mexicans hold border-crossing cards, known as *micas* because they are made of plastic. The *mica* allows the bearer to visit the United States for periods up to seventy-two hours. Although specifically prohibited from working in the United States, thousands use the *mica* as a passport to employment. Before dawn each morning at most border ports, thousands of *mica* holders pass through American gates on their way to work, returning to their homes in the evening. Thousands more remain on their jobs all week, crossing only on weekends — this group includes maids in private homes. One customs official in El Paso has three maids — at ten dollars a week each — who sleep in his basement.

To apply for a *mica*, a person has to show that he is a citizen of Mexico, that he has no intention of defecting, that he is of good moral character, and that he has been a resident of the area for not less than one year. His first step in acquiring a *mica* is to apply to Mexican Customs for Form 13, and this is where the *mordida* comes into play. In Tijuana they make a game of it, instructing the applicant to bring four pictures: two of himself and two of Hamilton or Jefferson or Washington, whatever the economics of the moment dictate. Of course, not all are that clever, but, amigo, who cares for jokes at a time like this — the bite is always painful.

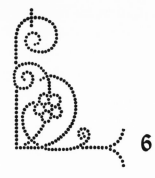

6

The Economics
of Narcotics

They call me a máquina, you know, a machine, a wheel; I make deals for Abdón Delgadillo, a teniente of David Cabrera, the jefe máximo in Mexicali. The guys who drive cars for me are called burros, mules. I bring up three-four tons of marijuana a month from Mazatlán, about five or six trips, and I get six thousand pesos a trip and the burros get three thousand pesos. We drive the cars, going first to Sonoita for our tourist permits, and sometimes Abdón flies down and meets us at the Hotel Regis in Mazatlán — there are always about fifteen or twenty buyers and sellers in this place. Everybody is quoting prices: thirty, forty, fifty pesos a kilo, but usually we say, "Well, let's see the merchandise." So we go to this small town called San

Marcos, where they grow nothing but marijuana in the mountains there. All they do in this little town is sell the grass; everybody there has some either in his home or in a barn or in a shack somewhere — all the farmers in the area have their little buildings in town. And everybody there is offering it; all the little children are running around and saying, "Come here, come here, come here. How many kilos are you going to take? My father sells it cheaper than anybody else." Some of the kids are pushing these little trucks with four or five bricks and others carry some in their arms, and they say, "Look at this. I will sell it to you cheap." All the trucks come in loaded — it looks like alfalfa — and they park in line on the street like they're going to market. The ones who don't have trucks use donkeys, and everyone is yelling, "Marijuana, marijuana, marijuana." There are soldiers there and the presidente of the municipio, the mayor, comes out and says, "Hey, come here. How many kilos are you going to take and who are you buying it from?" And then he'll tell you to go buy it from this person or that person. "I can get it much cheaper for you," he'll say. "And I can put it in Mazatlán for you."

When a guy arrives in San Marcos and he doesn't know the town or the area or anyone there, he goes to the mayor, or someone in the mayor's office, and they ask him how much he wants, two or three tons and so on. So they write him a little note and tell him where to go, and when he comes back he will show this little note to the soldiers, because he is not known, and they will pass him right on through. But me, I make my contact at the Regis, and I know where to go, and I give it a good look. It's all stacked up in kilo bricks and I take my machete and whack a brick in half to look at it. Then I grab another and whack it, too. If it has too much sugar in it I throw it down. They mix the marijuana with sugar — they dig a big hole and mix the two together with water. But when there's too much sugar, it's sticky and you can see the little specks, and it's kind of gritty, so I don't like it. Maybe, you know, they take three hundred pounds of marijuana and mix it with two hundred pounds of sugar and it makes five hundred pounds. Then in ten or fifteen days it gets white inside, and it doesn't look so good, and when you smoke it, it makes you cough. So I say, I want this stuff over there that hasn't been packaged yet. Then I can watch while they pack it and press it into bricks; then I'm sure there's not too much sugar in it. But you've got to stay there all the time or they might switch it on you in the end. Another thing is that good stuff won't have too much garbage in it, like seeds and stems; it's been de-loused and properly cured. Sometimes we sprinkle a little Coca-Cola or wine on it to keep it moist and it also covers the smell pretty good. Also the alcohol in the wine affects the salt and gives it an extra kick.

The good stuff costs about sixty pesos, which is what: four dollars and eighty cents? Business is very good now and when I tell the farmer I want five hundred kilos, he says, "Oh, hell, take a ton." I say, "Well, I don't have enough money for a ton." He says, "Take it anyway and *pay me when you sell it and come back down on your next trip." The sixty pesos include delivery in Mazatlán. They don't have to hide the marijuana down there, no secret compartments, or anything like that. They just load it in a truck and meet you someplace in Mazatlán, maybe in a field or woods outside town, where we make the transfer. You can put about six hundred kilos in the trunk of a '59 Oldsmobile. We jack the car up and put little blocks of wood between the springs and the frame and it keeps it real level. I usually take two or three cars, but when I take a truck, I go to Hermosillo and load up with produce and get it fumigated so I can get through the checkpoints. These are agricultural checkpoints and they are used also to prevent smuggling from the border from getting into the interior. So they are more interested in traffic going south than north. They put a seal on the truck in Hermosillo, and when you get to a checkpoint and they ask, "What are you bringing?" you say, "I'm bringing corn, tomatoes," you know, and they say, "Have they been fumigated?" and you answer, "Sure, here's the papers." Sometimes they raise the canvas top and look in there, but they don't punch any rods through or anything like that. When I take a big load of marijuana, like three or four tons, I load up with bananas. They're delicate, and the inspectors aren't going to push them around trying to find out what's on the bottom. . . .*

Marijuana literally grows like grass in many parts of Mexico. In states of high productivity (Nuevo León,

Tamaulipas, Aguascalientes, Durango, Jalisco, Chiapas, Sinaloa, Michoacán, Chihuahua, Sonora, Guerrero) it is very much a factor, though illegal, in the economy. Contrary to the protest of Mexican officials that production is being destroyed, the supply has managed to keep up with the increasing demand of recent years.

"It's a lost cause until you can control the demand," says Mayor López. "The problem is in the United States, not Mexico." Mexicans don't use marijuana or heroin? "No, we don't. No, we don't." You're just making everybody else addicts. "No, I think they are already made like that. I haven't even seen a marijuana cigarette, and I was raised here, and went to school here. I understand that in your schools even little children smoke marijuana and take pills and everything. The thing is, where do most of these young people in the United States get that stuff from? Do they come to Tijuana to get it? No, sir. They've got it right there in San Francisco, Los Angeles, Chicago, all over. How does it get there? Having the police force like you have, how is it possible to have so many drug addicts in your country? How is it possible? If we were to apprehend, right now, this minute, all the people who sell narcotics in Tijuana, all of them, tomorrow we would have new ones because there is money in it and there is a demand for it. This is what makes free enterprise, as you Americans call it."

This free enterprise enjoys remarkable economics. A kilo of marijuana, selling for $4.80 at the source, will regularly wholesale for $100 in Los Angeles and $200 in New

York, with a gamut of quotations in between. A famine ("panic" in ingroup argot) can double the price overnight. (The summer of 1969 saw the biggest panic in recent years, with the price soaring to $350 in Los Angeles — it was out of sight, literally, in New York's East Village.) The local profit scale includes big and small dealers, a variety of middlemen, and ultimately, the street pusher. There are approximately a thousand reefers in a kilo — at fifty cents to two dollars a stick, depending on the clientele, it makes for an attractive investment.

But even more attractive is Mexican heroin. If a kilo of eighty or ninety percent grade, costing from $10,000 to $12,000 at the source, is cut five times with a substitute (milk sugar, instant coffee, cocoa — Mexican heroin is brown) it will multiply into thirty-two kilos of approximately three percent potency, which is about the strength of junk dispensed on the streets of Eastern and Midwestern cities. Chances are it will be cut three or four times before it crosses the border, depending on the type of sale involved, and the American buyer will cut it as many times as the potency allows. The wholesale price in Baja California for ten to fifteen percent potency is $500 an ounce, or $17,000 a kilo. At the street level, it will retail at an average of five dollars a shot, for a return of about $20,000 per kilo of three percent stuff. But the total gross earnings of the original kilo is $640,000 (32 × $20,000). Obviously, the real profit is not in farming, but in smuggling and peddling, and nowhere is this more evident than along the border itself.

Joe F. Ray, a U.S. Customs agent who has spent a career chasing smugglers along the Mexican border (he headed the El Paso office before his retirement in 1968), was never overwhelmed by the efficacy of Mexican law enforcement: "The price of all narcotics is so high in Juárez that dealers in Tijuana could make money selling to dealers in Juárez. You can't buy marijuana for less than thirty-five dollars a pound (they use the pound measure here instead of the kilo) and junk will cost anywhere from six hundred fifty dollars an ounce on up. The reason for this condition is not great law enforcement, but a very effective system of extortion. Every time a smuggler turns around, someone is tapping him on the shoulder for the *mordida*. A lot of our big smugglers have defected to Mexicali and Tijuana in recent years. That's where the action is today. Juárez is known in the trade as a sorry place to do business in. Even dealers in Albuquerque, where there's quite a nest of junkies, will go to Tijuana, or even L.A., before coming to Juárez. Most of our traffic here comes from the interior. Dealers from the U.S. will go through Juárez on their way to Durango or Mazatlán or Aguascalientes, where there's a bunch of laboratories. But they don't even slow down for Juárez or El Paso. We've caught quite a few loads destined for Chicago that were picked up in these places."

This is pretty much the story along the entire border. For example, in fiscal 1969, customs agents stationed at ports in California and Arizona seized 20,910 kilograms of marijuana as opposed to 4,402 kilograms at Texas and

New Mexico ports. The ratio in heroin is more balanced: 13.6 kilograms for California-Arizona and 7.3 kilograms for Texas-New Mexico. This is principally due to European heroin coming through Veracruz and Tampico destined for Canada, Chicago and New York. The most fantastic growth has been in Tijuana, where 1961 seizures totaled 393 pounds of marijuana, 87 ounces of hard narcotics and 20,709 pills; in 1969, the seizures leaped to 20,332 pounds of marijuana, 534 ounces of hard narcotics and 5,022,526 pills.

Some of the largest seizures have come as complete surprises to customs agents, whose *modus operandi* is based primarily on informants and the reward system.

In 1963 an agricultural inspector in Laredo made the biggest "cold bust" in border history: seventy-six pounds of 99.6 percent pure heroin, worth at least twenty million dollars at street level. "It was just a fluke," says Gene Pugh, customs agent in charge in Laredo. "We have a hundred-percent baggage inspection here for anyone entering the United States. This Canadian couple drove in from Mexico City and were directed to secondary for a routine inspection. A coat was left on the rear seat, and when the inspector reached in, he noticed that the seat was very firm. His first thought was that it was packed with liquor. He removed the seat and found twenty-eight one-pound packages of heroin. So customs got real busy tearing that car down and found forty-eight more packages in the door panels. This couple had made two previous deliveries to Bridgeport, Connecticut, for the branch of the Mafia which operates between Canada, New York, and Marseilles, France, where the morphine base from Turkey is refined into heroin."

Another fluke in 1966 netted 1,325 pounds of marijuana when California fish and game wardens became suspicious of a raft being pushed ashore from a small boat anchored off Malibu. They thought they had found lobster poachers. On an average weekend there are thousands of small boats in Baja California waters, docking in and out of ports from San Diego to Los Angeles and points north. There are countless small airfields throughout the Southwest, and maps of Mexico's major marijuana- and heroin-producing states show hundreds of isolated airstrips.

The Los Angeles police have sniffers (informants) employed in the baggage departments of some airline terminals, who sniff the luggage of Mexican and Cuban subjects to detect marijuana, usually accomplished by compressing a suitcase with both hands and taking a deep breath. And that is only part of the problem. An estimated tourist exodus of twenty-four million in Tijuana and thirty-six million in Juárez pass through the ports every year, with forty thousand cars crowding the Tijuana gate on an average Sunday. Add to that a sixteen-hundred-mile border, with only a narrow, often dry river to mark Texas, where smugglers make boats by welding car hoods together. One smuggler, in his mid-seventies, swims across to Laredo with a pack of marijuana on his back. An invisible line on the California, New Mexico and Arizona borders separates the two countries, so you begin to appreciate the magnitude of the problem.

The means and ways of smuggling are infinite. The customs mail division in El Paso made five interceptions of marijuana in 1967 in quantities ranging from eight to sixteen ounces. The inspections were made because of other violations of postal regulations. "So what do you suppose is coming through the mails?" says Joe Ray. "The post office is very reluctant to open any first-class mail. My guess would be that a tremendous quantity of narcotics is entering the country in this manner. For example, we know that Manfredo Martínez, a fugitive from a narcotics rap in San Antonio, is mailing junk into this country from Ciudad Miguel Alemán, a small bordertown across from Roma, Texas. We caught fifteen ounces in one month. Martínez mails two and three grams of high-grade heroin in letters.

"A dealer here in Juárez was shipping marijuana by bus. The package we caught was addressed to a man in Pueblo, Colorado, an innocent bystander. I guess the intended receiver goofed, but the recipient was more than a little shocked at finding ten pounds of marijuana in his living room. Others ship it by freight train in a variety of containers. Last year a freight official in Lubbock, Texas, opened a carton that had been misdirected and found seven five-gallon cans of candy that turned out to be refined marijuana. We checked back on the shipment and found four more cartons, for a total haul of four hundred and twenty pounds. Trains move across the river here every day. Some cars are sealed before crossing into Mexico, and the others are subject to inspection when they return. But what's to stop a smuggler from hiding small quantities of junk under the train where there are innumerable hiding places, far too many for us to search on a daily basis. Frankly, we don't have that kind of manpower. We search very few people or automobiles coming through the gates. As an example, last month [November, 1967] the total number of people crossing on all three bridges was 2,947,624. Of this total, customs searched fourteen people in secondary and made six seizures. We got some pills, watches, and lighters, but no marijuana or heroin. Those are pretty good odds for traffickers: fourteen searched out of three million. I'm not talking about inspectors looking in the trunk or under the seats, but a strip job. You've got to have pretty good advance information before you go out and tear a car down to the rims. That's what it takes if you expect to find anything. They have pretty good bodymen over there. They build special traps in the fenders, underneath the car, in the door panels, or right in the frame or body itself. And there are so many places to hide something as small as junk: air cleaner, gas tank, tires, transmission, differential; you name it, they've tried it; in the walls of campers, or the butane container or refrigerator. We had a refrigerator truck come through here and found that the asbestos in the walls had been replaced with marijuana.

"Then what about pedestrians going back and forth every day; fat, old women with passels of kids, well-

dressed *turistas,* cute *señoritas,* friendly Mexican cops
and customs agents, diplomats with immunity, the thousands of American women who cross every day to shop or
visit beauty parlors, on foot and in cars, and the Mexicans
with border-crossing cards — how many are there right
here in Juárez? A hundred thousand? Two hundred thousand? Hell, I don't know, but I'll tell you, it's fantastic.
After a while a lot of these people get to know the
inspectors and become old friends: 'Good morning.'
'How're you today?' 'Fine, yourself?' 'Oh, just dandy.'
'Good-bye.' 'Bye-bye.' The inspectors would never dream
of pulling them into secondary. Some are bringing in
narcotics. You can bet on that. A little bit each day, and
that's the best type of operation. The smuggler doesn't
risk too much. If his mule is busted, he's lost only a few
ounces of junk or a pound or kilo of grass. It may not
seem like much would get across this way, but on a con-
tinual basis (by how many people?) it really mounts up
fast. And it goes on at all ports. It doesn't take much
figuring to see that we're far from controlling this situation. In fact, it gets worse each year. I constantly see
figures in magazines and newspapers about how customs
and the FBN [Federal Bureau of Narcotics] seize about
ten percent of the narcotics coming into the country. One
magazine last year gave the exact amount of heroin
smuggled into the country. I think it said a thousand
kilos. They even broke it down to a hundred and fifty
kilos from Mexico and the rest from Europe. How do they
do it? Well, they multiply the number of FBN's known

addicts by an average daily dose and arrive at a rough estimate. But nobody knows the number of addicts in this country, no more than we know the number of burglars. From my experience, I'd say the stuff being caught is so minute it's not worth guessing at. The only influence of customs everywhere has been to raise the salaries of carriers, and consequently the price of narcotics. It's not so much the quantity you catch that's important, but who. If you grab a big dealer with a few grams of heroin, it's more valuable than a mule with kilos. It's getting the people off the street that should be off the streets."

There are four checkpoints between Mazatlán and Mexicali. The first one is Benjamin Hill, which is about ninety miles north of Hermosillo. The next is Oasis, about halfway to the third point, Sonoita, on the Arizona border. The last one is San Luis, about forty-five miles from Mexicali. I never stop in San Luis or Oasis. They're just one-man stations and I zoom right on through. I laugh like hell when they blow whistles and scream and jump up and down in the road. When I'm driving for David Cabrera, I have no trouble at Benjamin Hill or Sonoita, because he's paid them off, you know — mordida. He used to pay ten thousand pesos a month to each checkpoint, but lately it's twenty thousand because he's a little hot right now. Sometimes I use his name when the stuff is for somebody else, but I don't like to do that too often. Now I will tell you about some of the things that have happened at checkpoints. One time I was coming up with

Enrique and another guy and we were each driving a car. I
was the first through the checkpoint, and I had six hundred kilos in the trunk of this Olds. The guard says,
"What are you carrying?" I says, "Nothing." He says,
"Open up the trunk," and I says, "I can't, I've lost the
key." So he grabs me by the shirt and says, "Then I'm
going to keep you here." So I says, "Wait, I'm going to
give you a little money." He says, "What are you carrying?" "It doesn't make any difference what I am carrying,"
I says. "That's what I'm paying you for, so I don't have to
show you." So I gave him fifteen hundred pesos and went
through. Now Enrique is coming up and he's real scared,
and then wham! He steps on the gas and shoots through
there at a hundred miles an hour. So the police jump in
their car and take off after him. Enrique is doing a
hundred and twenty and the first thing he knows his car is
heating up and cutting out on him, and he finally comes
to a stop. He jumps out and runs into the woods, and the
cops are right on his tail, shooting at him. And he's
returning the fire. While this is going on, the third car, a
Pontiac, gets through without any trouble. So I stop by
the police car and the cops are real mad that Enrique has
gotten away. They are mad because now they are stuck
with the car, which they have to take to their chief. If the
driver stays, you know, they can get some money out of
him, sometimes as high as ten thousand pesos. Lots of
times, though, when they catch a car and the driver gets
away, they steal some of the marijuana. I know that
Enrique had six hundred kilos and there was only two

hundred kilos left when they turned it in to their chief in Nogales. But if they know the driver's boss, they'll telephone and tell him to come get his load. There's a big trafficker in Tijuana called Lucky and his drivers once left two cars in Sonoita. They telephoned and when he got there his cars were in a service station near the checkpoint. He paid five thousand pesos for each car.

A while back, David Cabrera got mad at Abdón because he found out Abdón was cheating him on the price he was paying for the marijuana in Mazatlán. Abdón went to work for himself, and one day coming through the checkpoint in Sonoita he used David's name, and they said, "Wait a minute." They called David and asked him, and he said, "Hell, no, it ain't mine. Screw the guy, whoever the hell he is." And this was Abdón, and so he called me in Mexicali to bring some money and we paid them off, but they kept his Ford Ranchero. One time I played a good trick in Sonoita. I loaded my Olds down with potatoes and had three cars following with marijuana. So I went through the checkpoint and they chased me a few miles before I stopped, and they say, "Hey, what are you bringing there?" and I says, "Potatoes," and they say, "Yeah," and they opened the trunk and saw all those potatoes: "Hey, you can't take potatoes in Baja, that's prohibited." And they started hitting me up for the mordida, but I said, "I don't want them. You take them." They took all the potatoes and put them in their car and then my three load cars zoomed through and the cops *were so loaded down with potatoes they couldn't catch them. . . .*

A customs agent is only as good as his sources of information. "With good information," says Joe Ray, "you can knock off some of these people. But good information is hard to come by. We have informants on the other side who spend a great deal of time watching the homes of *known* smugglers. That's the key word — known. It's like the old saying: there's ten big dealers in Juárez — that's just ten *known* big dealers. There's probably twenty bigger ones nobody knows, but they just keep referring to the Big Ten. Coming back to our informants, if they spot a car leaving the lair of one of these known smugglers, they give us a call and we put the car's license number on the line and wait. Most of the time it never shows up, or if it does, it's clean. What happens is this. The smuggler is wise to this old trick. He uses two cars: the first for negotiations and the second to drive across in. It's a constant damn game. He may cross right behind the first car and the moment we pull it into secondary, he knows we've been had. Or, hell, we may tail it all the way to Albuquerque, hoping to bag the receivers. You see, in this business we seldom get amateurs. The big operators are hardened criminals with connections. In other lines of law enforcement, they get a lot of dumb bunnies trying their hand for the first time, but our kind start out sticking up gas stations and work their way up to narcotics. Oh, we get kids smuggling small amounts, but a lot of them get taken. If I had all the alfalfa we've caught here in the past year, I could start a dairy farm."

One U.S. Customs inspector at the Tijuana port described himself as a psychologist. "I watch for telltale signs," he said. "I look for perspiration on your forehead; I look at the veins in your neck to detect the pulse rate; I ask silly questions like 'Where were you born,' when all the time you look more American than I do. I want to hear the sound of your voice, not the answers. Is it weak, strong, perhaps too strong, and so on. If you try to be too friendly, or too helpful — for instance, if a guy comes through and says right away he's got a bottle stashed away under the seat, I say, ha, he's trying to tout me off the real thing, a little smokescreen. So I use the old psychology. I look for all these things. You try to be too friendly with me, too nice, too pleasant, too bold, too timid, anything abnormal, and you're in for a session in secondary."

When I come in with a load from Mazatlán, I take it to a ranch that belongs to Chew Willie — his name is Jesús Demara. I never have any dealings with David Cabrera. My teniente is Abdón, and David has a lot of tenientes like him. David is very well protected in all his dealings. He's got the money and the connections, the two most important things in this business. And he's been at it a long time and knows a lot of buyers from all over the country. In Mexicali, the deals are made at the Hotel Playa. That's where people looking for stuff get together. Let's say a buyer calls David and says, "I want five hun-

dred kilos." David says, "Okay, come down and get it next Wednesday." So Abdón meets them at the Hotel Playa and they agree on who furnishes the cars. If the buyer brings the cars down, Abdón will take them and turn them over to me or some other máquina, and we see that they are loaded and put in a certain place to be picked up. Abdón will then say they are ready and collect the money for them and they will be shot up to the United States. For this we need burros, but that's no problem. Abdón checks some guy out, you know, where he lives, how many kids, things like that, what kind of a guy he is, and whether he can be trusted. When he approaches him, he says, "Hey, this merchandise is not mine, it belongs to a guy over here, and he wants you to take it across for him." So later if something goes wrong, he can deny it. But it doesn't really matter, because David has paid for protection on this side, and Abdón is not crossing over. But if the burro skips out with the load, his family is in real bad trouble. If the buyer [American smuggler who peddles to wholesalers] takes delivery in Mexicali, the price runs between twenty and twenty-five dollars a kilo. Delivered in Calexico or Los Angeles or Las Vegas, it's about forty dollars. It depends on the arrangements, who furnishes the cars and drivers and so on. To have secret compartments built into the fenders and body of a car will cost about two thousand pesos. There are lots of garages in Mexicali that specialize in this type of work. . . .

Information for customs comes in a variety of packages. There is the small peddler (involved mostly with American

teen-agers and amateurs) who will inform on his customers for the reward — twenty-five percent of the value of any
smuggled goods recovered. Notorious in this league are
taxi drivers, bartenders, guides, pimps, and policemen —
that vast army of leeches that prey on the tourists. The
salaried informer lives in Mexico and spends his time
spying on known traffickers, often members of a ring he
works for; he keeps in contact by telephone and nerve-
wracking rendezvous; many are drug addicts. Ex-convicts
and others of dubious reputation, usually with relatives in
the United States, will turn informer to obtain a border-
crossing card. The largest group is made up of mules who
are busted in the United States and given a pass in
exchange for their cooperation.

"We don't burn a mule unless it's absolutely necessary," says a customs agent in Tijuana. "When we get
information that a load is coming through, we alert the
line not to touch it. At most ports a spotter on the other
side can see any car pulled into secondary. The spotter
will call his contact and he will call the pickup man at the
destination point and that's the end of it. So we pass it
through and make sure there's not a lieutenant in a chase
car following it. If there is, we lay back until he leaves.
He'll usually tail it a few miles to make sure everything is
all right before turning back. Our procedure is to follow
the mule to his destination, usually some sidestreet, where
he parks the car and leaves the keys in the ashtray. He
may leave a book or newspaper on the front seat for
identification. Then he calls his contact in Tijuana and
goes for a walk. The contact calls the pickup man, who

gets the car, takes it to a stash somewhere, unloads it, and brings it back to the same spot. Three or four hours later, the mule returns and drives back to Tijuana. What we do is pick up the mule after he's made his phone call, stake out the car, follow it to the stash, and bust everybody. Meanwhile, we've got the mule cooling his heels someplace else. Nobody knows we've got him. Maybe after he's thought about it a while in jail, he may decide to cooperate. If he does, we've got ourselves another contact. This is how we prefer to do it. Getting a mule is nothing. You get some poor, starving Mexican with a dozen kids who would do most anything for two hundred bucks. Our aim is to further the investigation and get the principals. So the mule takes the bus back to Tijuana and says, "Man, he never brought the car back. What happened?" He may be two days late, but time is not a factor in Mexico. A Mexican may show up for an appointment two weeks late and never mention it. It's not important. He's here now and that's it. Be grateful."

Muscle can be important in the recruiting of mules. "One day I heard through the grapevine of a certain grease monkey in Nuevo Laredo who had taken a load of marijuana to Chicago," says Gene Pugh, "and I went over there and told him to get in the car. I drove out of town and laid it on him. I said next time you go to Chicago, you better call me ahead of time if you want to come out of it with a whole skin. A month later, around three in the morning, there's a knock at my back door, and there's this guy. He says, 'Are you ready to go?' 'Go where?' 'Chicago.

I've got a hundred and twenty kilos of marijuana in the car and I'm on my way.' We drove to San Antonio where I picked up other agents, and we got a bale of hay and broke it up in this agent's living room and made a hundred kilo packages. We exchanged them for the marijuana, leaving the other twenty kilos intact. We followed him to Chicago in three cars. He made his telephone call, and the contact instructed him to wait, that he would be right down. So we told our man to take it easy if he had to follow the contact; we didn't want to lose them. Well, he stalled at every intersection until we were running over each other trying to stay out of sight. Finally, he drove down an alley and into a garage, and that's how we bagged Fats González, a big dealer in Chicago. I made three more trips to Chicago with the same informant before he got burned. In one two-year period, I made seventeen trips to Chicago."

Convoy surveillances seldom extend more than two hundred miles, unless — as in Pugh's Chicago trips — the mule driving the load car has agreed to cooperate, and even then the bulk of the marijuana is exchanged for alfalfa whenever feasible. A *cold* convoy of over two hundred miles was unheard of until September, 1967, when eight customs agents in four chase cars followed a load car with 522 kilos of marijuana from Calexico, California, to North Bergen, New Jersey.

"It was an information case," says John Van Diver, agent in charge in Calexico. "One of our agents, Paul Martin, learned about it through an informant. We knew the make of the car, the license number, approximately when it was coming through the port, and that it was headed back East somewhere. But that was all we knew. It was the most exhausting and frustrating — and yet the most exciting — trip I've ever taken. We had the load car under continuous surveillance for over three thousand miles, on freeways and tollways, through cities and side-streets and alleys, and didn't burn one car — they never knew we were there. None of us had any sleep or a hot meal in four days. By the time we reached New York state, we were all pretty punchy. And then when we discovered that the Bureau thought our informant was driving the load car, we really broke up. It sort of eased the tension. Imagine if we had lost it, all that marijuana — I don't even want to think about it. By the time we reached New Jersey, we had picked up eight more chase cars, and things got pretty well fouled up, with everybody on the radio yakking away — we couldn't get our messages through. At this point we felt, well, if you mothers screw us up we'll kill you. We didn't come three thousand miles to get fouled up at the end by some eager beaver in a hippie suit. Well, believe it or not, by the time we got to the delivery point there was one car left on the surveillance, and we were out of our skulls. Anyway, we made a good case and bagged three of the top men in the Cuban marijuana smuggling ring that operates between Mexico, Los Angeles, New York and Miami."

David Cabrera has the connection right at the top, both in Mexicali and Mexico City. When the city police and detectives give him trouble, he goes and raises hell with the big wheels. He says, "Look, I'm paying you so many thousand pesos a month and these guys are out here busting my people. Now, I want this straightened out." The federal prosecutor calls in the detectives or the chief of police in Mexicali and says, "Now, look. You guys don't work narcotics. This is a federal charge and a federal case and I want you guys to lay off of narcotics right now, because it's upsetting our investigation." There was this cop in the state judicial who was paid off and was still busting some of David's boys. Well, when they do this sort of thing, they don't last very long. This pistolero, El Cochito, got ten thousand pesos to knock him off. Lots of cops have been killed for this reason. But even a good cop gets knocked off if he makes too much trouble. First, David sends for him and says, "If you don't stop molesting my people, you are going to die. Here's some money and when you want more, let me know." Once they hear this, they know they better watch their step, because they will die if David wants them to die, and there is no getting around that. He's the jefe máximo; nobody fools around with him. . . .

The biggest *known* trafficker in Juárez is the legendary La Nacha (Ignacia Jasso de González), romanticized for nearly four decades as the queen of the border dope traffic. There is a *corrido* the *mariachis* sing in *cantinas* all over Mexico, one which tells the story of her husband, a mean *bastardo* called El Pabloti (Big Pablo) who was *muy macho*; he took nothing off anybody. When a policeman came into a brothel to arrest him one night, he said, "Pablo, you're coming with me." Pablo drew a gun and was killed in the exchange. La Nacha, who was in jail on a minor infraction, was permitted to attend Pablo's funeral and staged an impressive *escenita*, beating her breast and swearing vengeance. Today, in her eighties, she is still the border dope queen. In the intervening years, customs agents have expended a lot of energy trying to lure her across the border. The only respite in her career came during World War II, when the U.S. State Department applied pressure on Mexico to clean up the border for the thousands of troops stationed there. She was arrested as "an enemy of the peace" and lodged, without trial, in the maximum-security prison on Tres Marías Islands, sixty miles offshore in the Pacific.

She returned to Juárez after the war and resumed her career without further interruptions. Her connections in Mexico City, says Joe Ray, are as good as money can buy. She carries an *amparo*, which makes her immune to arrest, and it is renewed periodically by a judge. Besides narcotics, she operates a stolen-car ring and fences a variety of merchandise. She bankrolls marijuana and opium growers, and owns several laboratories which convert crude opium into heroin. "She's very fat, sort of an Indian type, squat, expressionless face, but highly intelligent," says Ray. "I've talked to her several times, and she's very frank about her business. Even though she's a woman, she's *muy macho*. She's been accused, and rightly so, of having had a number of people killed, and I know of two instances where she personally did the job."

Some of the finest hotels, restaurants, and brothels along the border, from Tijuana to Matamoros, are owned by narcotics traffickers, many of them fugitives from American justice — Mexicans with dual citizenship. Since the passage of the personal recognizance bond act, Mexican-Americans have been entitled to one "free fall." They sign a bond and jump across the border, where they automatically become citizens and are immune to extradition.

The Moderno Restaurant in Piedras Negras is widely known as the House Heroin Built. The El Rancho and Corona in Mexicali, two brothel-hotel-restaurant-nightclub combinations, are owned by a fugitive narcotics smuggler. Recently, in Mexicali, another trafficker-proprietor methodically chopped off his manager's fingers when he caught them in the till — without exciting the police.

"The attitude in Mexico is pretty much like it was in the United States during Prohibition," says John Van Diver. "You know, we felt it was a little crooked but kind of legitimate since so many respectable people wanted it. It's somewhat the same in Mexico today. The big dealers and buyers aren't really condemned. It's a tongue-in-cheek attitude. These guys have made huge fortunes and have large investments in legitimate enterprises, especially ranches. It seems that everybody in Mexico wants to own a ranch."

Gonzalo Nava is of the opinion that Miguel "Big Mike" Barragán, the biggest known trafficker in Tijuana, is a busy rancher. "Oh, yeah," says Nava, "he works the ranch; he works hard." Is he a good citizen? "Well, he's a man that minds his own business. You see, it's a funny thing. I know some of them guys and they are nice people. You see, they don't use it; they sell it. So they are passable people. But you can't make a friend of them, or people will think you belong to the same gang. The big problem is not here in Tijuana but down in the interior. And it's too bad, that's the only blame Tijuana gets — dope. Right here we can't even grow a flower. We have no water. If you come over here and see things from the bottom, you'll come to the conclusion that Baja California is a place that can't produce anything. Why, growing marijuana takes more water than you can believe. The big problem is the easy transportation. President Alemán made highways all over. He made a highway that takes you from here to Mexico City in forty-four hours on the bus for only seventeen-sixty one way. So he makes an opportunity for these people in the interior to come over here and try to get rich overnight."

Barragán has "dumped a lot of people," police say. In fact, he allegedly maintains his own burial grounds in the desert south of Tijuana. Occasionally, he decides on cremation (setting the corpse on fire with gasoline) as a means of dramatizing his philosophy of "live and let live." Deported to Mexico in 1949 after serving two years in the federal penitentiary on McNeil Island in Puget Sound, Barragán today lives in exclusive Colonia Chapultepec, a next-door neighbor of the chief of consular services in the American consulate. He owns a ranch in Valle de Las

Palmas, the El Camino Bar in Tecate, and extensive real estate in Tijuana, including an unfinished six-story hotel. Among his closest associates are Juan and Roberto Hernández, also American fugitives, who are considered major traffickers by the Federal Bureau of Narcotics and the state of California. Questioned in Tijuana in 1961 by U.S. Customs officials, following a gun battle with police in which he was wounded and an informant was killed, Barragán asserted he did not drink, smoke or take narcotics; he would be unable to distinguish morphine from flour; he had never even seen marijuana, opium or any other narcotics; and the Hernández brothers were total strangers. In April, 1968, Barragán was again involved in a "shoot-out" with U.S. and Mexican federal police — heroin valued at three hundred thousand dollars was found in his possession.

The life of an informant can be perilous, as Robert Corenevsky discovered in 1963, when his old prison pal Roberto Hernández invited him to join his narcotics ring. A parole violator from the United States, Corenevsky decided that a little information to Customs would earn him points toward his future repatriation. Through various rendezvous and telephone calls, Corenevsky outlined the Hernández operation. Cruz Macías and Mike Barragán were frequent visitors at the Hernández household, and the wives of all these men were busily engaged in the traffic. Corenevsky did manage a free trip to Mexico City by telling Barragán that he knew a girl at the Cuban Embassy who was in charge of the cocaine distribution. Barragán gave him money to obtain a sample, and Corenevsky neglected to tell him the girl had been recalled to Cuba until he returned from his holiday. In the Hernández operation, he told Customs, a buyer from the United States would first go to the home of Miguel Sarabia in Colonia La Mesa to examine the merchandise and pay half of the money. The narcotics were then transported to the Hernández residence, which was owned by Barragán, and the method of conveyance into the United States was decided. The shipment to the border was under the supervision of Alfonso Soto, a Tijuana policeman. On October 9, 1963, a letter from a Mr. Smith in Tijuana advised customs of Corenevsky's fate: "Here is his papers. He made one phone call too much. Our regets to his widow."

"Some years ago I was with the Mexican Secret Service in Tijuana," says an informant, "and I got to know Cruz Macías pretty well. On several occasions he asked me to do jobs for him, but I always refused. One time he wanted me to take a load of machine guns, rifles and handguns to Sinaloa, for he had a deal to swap them for heroin. Then he wanted me to smuggle narcotics into the United States for a hundred dollars a trip. He had a very good business. Sometimes on weekends four or five customers would arrive at the same time. Then one day I was a little short, so I shook down one of his customers for forty dollars. The next day I was brought before the chief of the State Judicial Police in Tijuana, who took my badge and credentials and said I was finished in Baja California as a policeman. You see, the procedure set down for the *mor-*

dida is that all officers are required to bring a prisoner to the station where everybody can get a piece of him. The chief never mentioned Macías or anything. It was just good-bye, but not good luck."

"I had a half-assed informant," says Gene Pugh, "a guy who never produced but always promised. He had served eight years in Leavenworth and was a fugitive living in Mexico. So one day he's coming down a mountain with six hundred kilos of marijuana and missed a curve. His partner was pinned in the wreckage, so this guy takes a rock and finishes him off. He was convicted, sent to jail, then killed two guards while escaping. He now lives in Nuevo Laredo. They're in no hurry to bust him. The longer he stays out, the more he'll pay. It's a cash-on-the-barrelhead philosophy of law enforcement. I've worked with these people for many years, but I'm not deluding myself. If they ever got me in that jail, they'd cut my balls off."

There is a joke in Tijuana about trafficker Patricio Becerra Ortiz, a sadistic homosexual, having had to kill a policeman so he could get in jail where business is conducted for less *mordida*. He currently operates from a privately owned trailer in La Mesa prison south of Tijuana. In 1967 Salomón "El Tutu" Sández, another fugitive dealer, died of an overdose of heroin in La Mesa. When Cruz Macías was in La Mesa in 1965, U.S. Customs made several narcotics seizures by merely staking out the prison and taking down license-plate numbers of visitors who were later arrested at the port.

Corruption is not exclusive to the Mexican side of the line. Roy Ávila Villanueva, police chief of Alamo, Texas, was convicted of narcotics violations in 1964 — he made four separate sales to undercover federal agents. Ávila's troubles began when he found the name of an alleged New Orleans narcotics dealer on the person of a suspect, whom he released on a promise he would never return to Alamo. Ávila then sent a telegram to the New Orleans dealer, offering to sell two kilos of oranges at a bargain price. As it turned out, the New Orleans dealer was a federal agent.

Everybody has his little movida *in heroin. You can't trust nobody with junk. It's too easy to cut and who's to know what happened except the guy himself. What's David going to do: give a* teniente *fifty thousand dollars and say go get me five kilos of heroin? No, no, never. He flies down to Culiacán and buys it himself. He may stay there a week and watch them cook the* goma *into heroin. That's the only way he can know for sure what he's getting, how pure it is and all that. Some dealers take a hype along and have him shoot it up, but that's no good. You can smell it, or look at it for traces of a cutter, but you don't really know how good it is unless you get a chemist to analyze it. A carrier brings it back to Mexicali, but David has his eye on him all the time. And it goes right into David's house or a special hiding place. Sometimes dealers get together on a big buy and split it up, but they're not going to trust many other people. Now, I'll give you Chew Willie's action. He works for Abdón and peddles to street pushers and shooting galleries and American kids. He picks up guns and cars in trade, and they are shipped down to Sinaloa or Durango or some other place in the interior, where they'll bring ten times what they do here. Stolen cars and guns is big business in Mexico.*

A gun, you know, is muy macho *out in the hills there in the interior. You see some kid there on the street and he's got an M-1 strapped to his side and he's a real big deal, just a young kid. If a cop sees him with the gun, he's not going to pay any attention to him, because he knows he'll kill him before he gives it up. He's not going to come over and say, "Give me the gun, you don't have a permit." Nobody is going to give a gun away. A lot of the farmers are very poor, they live in these little* jacales, *and they need guns to protect themselves against the* bandidos *who roam the mountains there, always looking to get some money somewhere. Even the women will use the guns and it's pretty hard on the* bandidos *if they've got good weapons. The farmers have to defend themselves. They can't call the police. If a farmer is raising marijuana or the poppy, and some guys come and rob him, what is he going to do? He can't report to some cop sitting on the corner having a beer: "Hey, I've just been robbed." They've got to protect themselves, and that's one of the reasons they like the guns so much. . . .*

Long before the Chinese introduced the opium poppy into Mexico, American farmers had had their fling with it.

There was a time in this country when opium and morphine were as common as aspirin and recommended for as many ailments. Opium was peddled in a variety of patent medicines, and doctors prescribed it for everything from melancholia to constipation. At the turn of the century, heroin was introduced as a new miracle drug and Bayer was the first to package it. Statistics then estimated the ratio of drug addiction as one in every hundred — a half-million addicts. The files of the Federal Bureau of Narcotics currently list the names of some sixty thousand known active addicts, a figure believed so underestimated by many authorities as to be meaningless.

The Mexicans learned the value of the poppy from the Chinese. For many years the population of northern Mexico was heavily Oriental; and opium dens flourished, not only on the Mexican side, but along the California coast all the way to San Francisco. Opium was sold in five-*tael* (six-ounce) brass cans with a picture of two roosters on the label.

In the early Thirties, the Chinese were expulsed from Sinaloa, Sonora and Chihuahua, and many wealthy Chinese were reduced to poverty overnight. "Importers and merchants in Sonora, alone, will lose upward to $10 million," the New York *Times* reported on September 4, 1931. "Now, Chinese crossing the line at Naco asserted that they were charged prohibitive prices by Mexican immigration officers for permits to leave the country. . . . Those unable to purchase the permits . . . were stripped of all their clothes except their trousers."

("When a Chinaman died, you never found any passport or papers," a retired customs inspector recalled. "The family immediately sold them to the highest bidder.")

Of all the climates suitable to the temperament of the opium poppy, the Chinese preferred the thin dry air of the Sierra Madre Occidental, which rises from the Gulf of California in the small state of Sinaloa. Today the poppy grows in Sonora, Chihuahua, Durango, Jalisco and many other states. Like marijuana, it has become a factor in the economy.

Testifying before a subcommittee headed by Senator Thomas Dodd, customs agent Lee Echols told of a 1962 trip to Culiacán, capital of Sinaloa, with a group of Senate investigators, and of their introduction to an opium dealer. "We told him that we had heard the Mexican government was destroying the crops, but he assured us this was not so. The trafficker said that whenever Mexican officials destroyed opium poppies, it was either a small field that had been planted for that purpose or larger fields after the opium had been extracted. . . . I made an investigation there in 1953 and obtained the names of most of the people in the higher echelon of the opium and heroin traffic. One of these men was the Mayor of Mocorito."

Each year the Mexican Government announces the destruction of many acres of marijuana and poppies before the United Nations, and each year the United States contributes millions of dollars to this program. Although the Federal Bureau of Narcotics has praised this effort, the actual results to date have been less than impressive.

Equally unimpressive was Operation Intercept, described by U.S. officials as the largest peacetime search-and-seizure operation ever conducted by civil authorities (while it lasted). Launched on September 21, 1969, it introduced Mexican businessmen to an economic boycott unparalleled since 1929 when President Hoover placed a six o'clock curfew on Americans visiting bordertowns. At that time the Mexican Government retaliated by limiting the movement of U.S. trains to the same curfew restrictions, which immobilized them for twelve hours each day. The plan was soon abandoned.

Operation Intercept was designed to awaken the Mexican Government to its responsibility in the narcotics traffic. The Nixon Administration was demanding a two-pronged attack: (1) the destruction of marijuana and poppy fields, and (2) the arrest and prosecution of bordertown traffickers responsible for most of the narcotics flowing across the border. Until these terms were met, the United States was committed to continue to impede traffic at border ports. At some ports, the traffic was backed up for miles and with delays as long as six hours. No border official believed that cursory inspections, two to three minutes per vehicle, would seriously reduce the supply of narcotics moving across the sixteen-hundred-mile border. It was, as businessmen on both sides of the border loudly protested, blackmail, pure and simple. President Gustavo Díaz Ordaz called it a "bureaucratic blunder" that has "raised a wall of suspicion between my country and the United States."

On October 10, after three days of talks in Washington between U.S. and Mexican officials, it was announced that "the United States will adjust its procedures for inspections at the border in order to eliminate unnecessary inconveniences, delays and irritations." The two governments agreed to work out "an agenda to deal more specifically not only with present narcotics and marijuana problems but also with more immediate solutions." The statement said both countries had agreed to "readopt the joint communiqué which resulted from talks held in Mexico City on June 9–11, in which they pledged to cooperate in their mutual efforts to combat the overall drug problem." Mexico also agreed to "continue intensifying its own enforcement against illicit production and traffic of narcotics, marijuana and other dangerous drugs." This was interpreted by U.S. diplomatic sources to mean that Mexico would police the border against dangerous drugs as vigorously as the United States. Consequently, Operation Intercept had not failed. On the contrary, U.S. officials asserted, it had achieved the objective of getting Mexico to promise a greater role — Operation Intercept was now Operation Cooperation.

When the soldiers go into the mountains, they go see the presidente *of the* municipio *first, and he goes into the mountains with them. He's the one who talks to the farmers. He says, "Give me a little money to protect you*

here." Then he goes to the commandante who sent the
soldiers and pays him. The soldiers go into the mountains
and find fields of marijuana and poppies that are no good,
not enough water, rotten, or just stalks after the harvest,
and they burn that; and it comes out in the newspapers
and people say, "Look, the soldiers burned a lot of stuff."
It shows the soldiers are fighting this, and the government
gets more money from the United States. When the
soldiers come, they usually have to stay ten or fifteen days
so they can create the impression they have been doing
some good searching. Sometimes the farmers and soldiers
get into fights and kill each other. Back in 1966, fifteen
soldiers were killed one night while they slept, and this
friend of mine, Juan Tostado, killed five of them himself.
This time the soldiers had burned a lot of good marijuana
and poppies. The soldiers charged the farmers so much
money to protect them, and then came back after the
crops were grown and wanted more money, quite a bit
more. The way it was, they made a deal; like a farmer
would say, "Let me grow on this land and I will give you
five or ten thousand pesos." They made the deal and the
money was paid; but when it was time to harvest, the
soldiers came back and said, "If you don't give me forty
thousand pesos, I'm not going to let you sell one kilo of
this. I'm going to burn it off." So all the farmers got mad
and ganged together; they got guns and rifles, and fought
to protect their crops. This Juan who killed the five
soldiers, he was telling me that after the killings the
farmers couldn't go into town for a couple of months. So

they got together and they sent a fellow undercover to make a deal with the soldiers. It was arranged and they paid more money and things were straightened out.

Back in the Thirties and early Forties, in the days before the San Diego press discovered the economics of tourism and the minus factor of a bad image, there were great blood-and-thunder stories that told of "opium dens . . . powerful rival gangs . . . open battlefields . . . completely corrupt politics." Even the Tijuana press (i.e., that small segment of it not on the *mordida*) got into the act. The "crime and drug traffic," said one newspaper, "has a stranglehold on Governor Taobada." This story landed three reporters in jail. The San Diego press leaped to their defense, and President Ávila Camacho ordered their release and recalled Taobada to Mexico City under technical arrest. It was later charged that drug traffickers had helped put Taobada into office. The new governor, Juan Rico, was "shocked by the border crime situation." He imported a federal investigator and appointed a new police chief to replace the old one, who was in jail for killing a lawyer who had dared criticize his active connection with the drug traffic. The two biggest narcotics rings "operated openly" and the leaders were "headstrong, arrogant and careless." One of the leaders, Enrique Diarte, was described as a "Robin Hood–type character," and the other, Pancho "The King" Orbe, as a "sullen, ugly man with a long criminal record." The big American buyer was "the brother of a former Chicago district attorney, a

limping man nicknamed 'Step and a Half.' " As events
unfolded, Diarte was killed and Orbe was charged with
his murder; Step and a Half was apprehended with a large
quantity of American money, a serious crime in Mexico
in wartime. A few policemen were discharged, and life
soon returned to normal.

Today, with the tremendous acceleration of the narcotics traffic in Baja California, brown Mexican heroin
supplies most of the Pacific Coast and Southwest. Although not as skillfully refined as white European heroin
(impurities make it brown, sometimes almost black) and
certainly not as potent when it leaves the laboratory
(European heroin will test in the nineties, Mexican in the
eighties), it has earned a reputation with junkies for its
potency on the street — which simply means it has not
been cut as many times with a substitute. Sharp operators
will cut European heroin with cocoa or instant coffee and
pass it off as Mexican. They aim to please. Deaths from
overdoses have increased in recent years — a common
result when a junkie with a "needle habit" who is used to
highly adulterated drugs gets a shot of potent Mexican
stuff. Much of the junk on Midwestern and Eastern streets
will test not more than two or three percent, while in
California it runs five or six, and sometimes as high as ten
percent.

One explanation offered by police for the street potency
of Mexican heroin is the absence of Mafia controls in its
distribution. It is true that few Mafia-connected traffickers
have been apprehended with Mexican heroin, but this

supposition is not entirely accurate on two important counts: first, Mafia activities abound in many of these areas, and second, the Federal Bureau of Narcotics, which has been responsible for most Mafia narcotics arrests, has not been as active along the Mexican border. There are only two agents in San Diego, working as liaison with the Mexican federal police. The only other office is in San Antonio, a hundred fifty miles east of Laredo, and its small staff is unknown to most U.S. Customs agents on the Texas border. Cooperation between the two bureaus has not been ideal: FBN is opposed to customs's reward system and customs is opposed to FBN's undercover buys, claiming that small pushers are sometimes financed into the upper echelon of trafficking. (In April, 1968, the Bureau of Narcotics and the Bureau of Drug Abuse Control were abolished, and the Bureau of Narcotics and Dangerous Drugs of the Department of Justice was created in its place.)

Pondering the smuggling dilemma, Joe Ray offered a solution: "If we could only find a bug in the marijuana that endangers, let's say, the petunia crop in the United States, you'd find the farmers organizing to protect their crops from that bug; and we would get a lot more appropriation, better equipment, more personnel; and we'd do a much more effective job."

The belief in California is that any man with imagination, loot, wheels, and balls can start his own little syndicate and live happily ever after in suburbia — the astronomical profit guarantees the American Dream. But some, equally ambitious, have landed in riverbed shacks with their throats cut and their pockets turned inside out. Mexican traffickers learned long ago that there is even more profit in stealing. Others end up in Mexican jails, which more often than not is another form of stealing — Mexican police are notoriously accurate in judging a prisoner's ability to pay. The laws are flexible and their execution is leisurely; the defense attorney is allowed up to a year to prepare his case, and narcotics offenses are not bailable. It usually will not take more than a day in a Mexican jail for an American's anxiety rate to zoom up into the reckless zone. After a week, he will gladly liquidate his soul, as well as his American Dream, to gain his freedom. In Mexico there is usually a pecuniary logic behind the pervading madness; in the penal system, it has been refined into an art, as any former lodger will fervently testify.

The ingenuity of smuggling knows no bounds. "If we have good information on a suspect and can't find anything, we'll take him to the hospital for a flush job," says a customs inspector. "This is perfectly legal; lots of case law gives us the right to search a person's body cavities. Of course, we need probable cause, but it's part of the border search which involves everybody coming in from a foreign country. We can make a person disrobe for a visual examination, but we can't go probing around. For that we need a medically clean atmosphere and medical personnel. Frankly, the visual examination is not too valuable. I've had lots of people spread their cheeks and never saw a thing, then a doctor comes along and pulls out two ounces of junk tied up in a contraceptive. Sometimes it can be quite a job getting it out if it's in there far enough, and it's dangerous. But not as dangerous as the characters who swallow it. Here's the way it works. The first thing the buyer will do is get a room on both sides of the border. He buys an ounce of heroin from a peddler, takes it to his room over there, pulls out a bunch of small balloons, about the size of your small finger, and spoons in about two grams per balloon, ties off the neck of the balloon, clips the excess rubber, and ends up with fourteen round little balls, which he swallows with water. He hurries to his room over here, sticks his finger down his throat, and re-gurgitates an ounce of junk. About a ten-minute opera-tion from the time he swallows to when he brings it up. A very common procedure. These guys are out there try-ing to beat you all the time."

Addicts living in American bordertowns can walk across the line and get a shot at a local shooting gallery for as little as a dollar. The law requires that addicts register with Customs before entering Mexico, and though thou-sands do register each month, Customs believes it is only a small percentage of the actual number entering Mexico for that purpose.

Each year tens of thousands of American teen-agers come to the border for action. They find it in psychedelic freak-out joints, where pot and pills are dispensed like pop-corn. Most pills, including amphetamines and barbitu-rates, are available in drugstores without a prescription, usually at a lower price than in the United States with a prescription. They are not illegal in Mexico. "In our law they are not considered narcotics," says Mayor López. "Some of them are new and the health authorities haven't had the chance to go to Mexico City to include them inside our laws." Meanwhile, it is a multimillion-dollar business.

Since nobody knows how many heroin addicts there are in the United States, it follows that nobody knows how much junk is coming in from foreign countries. The estimates start with FBN's 60,000 known active addicts and spiral up — in the opinion of experts — to a half million. (In New York City alone, two hundred and fifty users, average age twenty-two, died of heroin overdoses or poisoning in the summer of 1969.) If the latter figure were cut in half, and each of the 250,000 addicts nursed a mild habit of four grams a day, it would equal a metric ton, or 365,000 kilos annually. On the street, it would retail for $7.3 billion, and that can buy a lot of dreams — in suburbia and in limbo.

Once I heard there was some real old marijuana way up in the mountains that I could get at a good price. You've got to be muy macho to go up into the hills there in Sinaloa. I got a Jeep and a couple of fellows, and we went to see these people. The marijuana was about a year old and very dry and it was at harvest time; they were cutting brand-new stuff right then, so I figured I could get it pretty cheap. When we got there the farmers had their guns out, and we took our weapons out, and everybody stood around and talked with the guns cocked in their hands. That was to make sure there wasn't going to be any robbery or bad deals. So nobody better try nothing funny. We got eight hundred kilos and ended up paying the usual sixty pesos because it turned out to be pretty good stuff, dry and not too much smell to it. You can smell fresh marijuana everywhere. Well, anyway, that's the way business is conducted up in the mountains. . . .

7

Señor Tijuana
Is Gringo

Back a millennium, back in the good old uncomplicated days of bathtub gin and caviar, when prizefighters and movie stars were the nation's alter ego, there was a retreat a few miles south of Tijuana where anyone, for mere pieces of gold, could regain Paradise. They called it Agua Caliente.

But even then, not everyone was impressed with the virtues of Paradise: a large sign proclaimed the sixteen-mile stretch from San Diego to Tijuana the "Road to Hell" (one commuter later changed it to "A Hell of a Road"), and Tijuana itself was branded the "wickedest city in the world." Of course, this was a first-rate line of advertising. "A stranger in any Northwestern small town," one American writer observed, "could get admitted to full membership in the local sporting set, with credentials to all whiskey peddlers and a reserved gunnysack in all hay-mow poker games, merely by proving that he had been to Agua Caliente." They came by the thousands, by all means of locomotion, to see what Paradise in the midst of Hell was really like. They found a green and flowered oasis in the middle of a desert.

Motoring up a dusty road, the visitor would make a sharp left turn, and there before him was Agua Caliente in all its dazzling white, red-topped glory, nestled in a bed of exotic shrubs and flowers, stately palms, immaculate lawns and formal gardens. To the left was the hotel, and to the right, beyond a small courtyard and a wishing well, was the casino, and beyond that the cabaret restaurant, said by many (and often) to do credit to the Café de Paris at Monte Carlo. There was a spa, swimming pools, tennis courts, a championship golf course, gift shops, and stables with five-gaited saddle horses. The cuisine was epicurean, and the finest wines and liquors of Europe came through the port at Ensenada.

"Agua Caliente was like a dream," says Tijuana historian Roberta Ridgely. "It gave you a sense of isolation and unreality that you'll never find again. It was a beautifully reconstructed idea of what a Spanish estate might have been like but never was. But you can't believe everything that was written about Agua Caliente. Much of it was terribly exaggerated. It's not true that all the tropical birds had their own valets."

Gonzalo Nava worked at Agua Caliente when it first opened in 1928. "I used to serve drinks at the gaming tables. Oh, I used to make money like a fool in those days. Later on I became a dealer and made even more money. People were going crazy with money. They couldn't get enough of the gambling; they'd complain because we closed for five hours, from five in the morning till ten. My God, I'd love for you to have seen that place for just one hour. Agua Caliente was something you wouldn't believe unless you saw it. They had every kind of gambling imaginable: craps and poker, blackjack, faro, chuck-a-luck, roulette, slot machines, everything. The main casino was huge, and there was the Gold Room for high stakes. They had a special room where you paid fifty dollars for dinner, and everything was gold. High rollers like Carl Laemmle and Joe Schenck used the gold service for their private parties. Of course, the movie stars were there all the time. All the big ones, like Gary Cooper, Clark Gable, Gilbert Roland, John Barrymore, Charlie Chaplin, Lupe Velez, Ricardo Cortez, Warner Baxter, Al Jolson, Wallace Beery, Tom Mix, Douglas Fairbanks, Mary Pickford, Norma Talmadge, Buster Keaton, Mabel Normand, Gloria Swanson, Hal Roach, Harold Lloyd, Jean Harlow — my God, she was a regular over there. They came for a good time, you know; a lot of them left their wives or husbands at home, and would bring a friend instead. We used to call it the Hollywood whorehouse. Rita Hayworth started there when she was just a little girl, dancing with her father, Mr. Cansino, who was the biggest drawing card there. We got all the best people: Jack Dempsey, Barney Oldfield, Babe Ruth — it was a very high-class operation. There was so much call for champagne they packed it in trash-cans to keep it cool. Oh, I tell you, Agua Caliente was the most tremendous thing that ever happened to Tijuana. Las Vegas is just cheap stuff."

Besides movie and sports personalities, Agua Caliente attracted the high rollers of the world. Ships were com-missioned from Monte Carlo to bring European gamblers, and in the States it was *de rigueur* for all gamblers to try their luck at the casino.

The creators of Agua Caliente were three American entrepreneurs and one enterprising Mexican general: Wirt G. Bowman, mentioned in Chapter 2; Baron Long, a San Diego innkeeper; James Crofton, an Oregon gambler and bootlegger, and Abelardo Rodríguez, governor of the Ter-ritory of Baja California del Norte, and celebrated as Obregón's fighting favorite. Built on land owned by Ro-dríguez, Agua Caliente originally cost seven million dol-lars; in the next few years, the hotel was enlarged fivefold, and two additions were tacked onto the casino.

Born in 1889 of indigent parents in Guaymas, Sonora, Rodríguez's career was considered humble (he made and sold artifacts) until he joined the revolutionary forces of Venustiano Carranza, Alvaro Obregón and Plutarco Elías Calles and became a "finger general" — a revolutionary practice of pointing a finger at a man and saying: "You, be general; you, colonel; you, private. . . ."

Rodríguez's colleagues at the time of his appointment

to the governorship of Baja in 1920 were the most powerful men in Mexico. Carranza served as provisional president from 1917 to early 1920, at which time Obregón and
Calles accused him of reactionary leanings and declared
against him. Carranza fled toward Veracruz with as much
of the government treasury as he could carry, but never
made it — he was murdered in his sleep by a guerrilla
under orders from Colonel Lázaro Cárdenas, also presidency bound. Elected president in November, Obregón,
often arbitrary and brutal, went down in history as a
dictator. Murdered by a religious fanatic in 1928, he was
succeeded by another dictator, Calles, who (not unlike
the hated Porfirio Díaz he had fought against) killed
all enemies he could not buy.

However successful in war and politics, Rodríguez's
greatest achievements were in the realm of high finance.
For example, in 1955, when he sold only part of his
Mexican holdings, it was reported to be the biggest banking transaction in the history of Mexico; even then he
retained all of his foreign assets and most of his interests
in Baja California. His first important financial move as
governor of Baja was the purchase of a large parcel of land
from Alejandra Argüello, one of many heirs to a grant
deed of 26,027 acres known as Rancho de Tijuana, which
included the 2,065-acre plot later integrated as the city of
Tijuana. First granted to Santiago Argüello in 1829 by
José María de Echandía, governor of the Province of Baja
California, the deed was sanctioned in 1861 by President
Benito Juárez. Following the death of Santiago in 1879,
President Díaz presented his widow with a new title.

Everything at Agua Caliente was done with a dollar-sign flourish. The 1930 Agua Caliente Open was the biggest-money golf tournament in the world at twenty-five thousand dollars, and this in the first year of the depression. The Caliente racetrack, also built on land Rodríguez had purchased from the Argüello heir, opened that same year and its top handicap was one hundred thousand dollars.

By then Rodríguez was back in Mexico City, where he served as minister of industry, commerce and labor a few years before his old friend Calles (who was still *jefe máximo*) "finger pointed" him into the presidency after he had "finger pointed" Órtiz Rubio out of it. Rodríguez completed the last two years (1932 to 1934) of Rubio's term.

Lamberto Parada drove an armored car for Banco del Pacífico in Tijuana in the early Thirties. He would pick up specified amounts from Agua Caliente three times a week; the rest went to the Bank of Italy in San Diego. "They had just a small account in our bank, mostly to pay local bills and for the payoff to Mexico City. I know about the payoffs because I saw the trade acceptances go out of there every single week — two hundred thousand and three hundred thousand pesos every time. That's how the gamblers paid for the concession. That was the *mordida*."

Agua Caliente was not all champagne and caviar. It anticipated Las Vegas as a volume operation. Lunch was a dollar, and a weekend "package deal" included wine with dinner. As many as ten thousand visitors passed through its portals on an average day, and the racetrack drew

crowds of up to a hundred thousand over a weekend. The
"take" on an average weekend was reported at five hundred thousand dollars; but it apparently was not enough,
for they began to steal the sweepstakes. Eventually, Baron
Long was barred from the track and quit racing; James
Crofton was barred from nearly every track in the United
States. The operation got so loose that even the Shelton
gang of southern Illinois tried to muscle into it. These
elements of corruption, creeping in at the time, have
given the Caliente racetrack its questionable reputation, a
stigma that has persisted to this day.

The repeal of Prohibition did not affect its business. At
Agua Caliente, the 1920's never died; the same frantic
pace went on until 1935, the year President Cárdenas
banned gambling throughout Mexico. The racetrack and
casino were padlocked on July 22, 1935. Calles, who had
an interest in several gambling houses, tried to organize a
coup d'etat against Cárdenas, but it failed and he was
exiled.

For the next two years, sporadic rumors, often backed
by news stories, circulated to the effect that Cárdenas had
modified his edict to permit gambling in the territories of
Baja California and Quintana Roo. The casino never
reopened; the union seized it for unpaid wages. Later it
was converted into a school and gradually allowed to
deteriorate to a stage where today it resembles more an
Aztec ruin than a latter-day Paradise.

Horseracing was legalized in 1937, and a long list of
operators took turns at running the Caliente racetrack,

each with a hope of recapturing the golden years, but all failed — the Depression had finally caught up with even the small spenders. When prosperity, in the guise of World War II, began lining the pockets of defense workers, the lucky operator was Eddie Nealis, a Los Angeles gambler and a onetime partner of gangster Bugsy Siegel in the Clover Club on Los Angeles's Sunset Strip. With the competition in the United States (Santa Anita, Hollywood Park, Del Mar) closed for the duration, Caliente was back in action.

Meanwhile, eight Argüello heirs were contesting the sale of their joint property by one heir to Rodríguez. Included in the petition was a challenge to the constitutionality of a "null and void" decree issued in 1929 by President Emilio Portes Gil, which had declared the land a patrimony of the nation. The case was before the Supreme Court throughout the war years. In December, 1945, the court ruled in favor of the heirs and a new group took over the racetrack.

Augustín Silveyra, a Tijuana businessman who had represented the heirs in Mexico City, became general manager of the racetrack. "I spent four years fighting the case in Mexico City and they gave me twenty-five percent of the stock and put me in charge of the actual operation." Did you need backers in Mexico City? "Well, you always need the right people in Mexico City to operate anything. I had some very good backers. There was General Rafael Ávila Camacho, the brother of President Manuel Ávila Camacho [in office from 1940 to 1946];

General Rodrigo Quevedo, a former governor of Chihuahua and a very rich man; Enrique Parra, then head of the
Foreign Bank — all these men were political powers in
Mexico City; and Gonzalo Gonzáles, who you might call a
'front' — they gave him seven percent to represent them.
The name of the corporation was changed to Hipodromo
de Tijuana, but the track was still called Caliente. We got
a gambling permit that was good for ten years, but in
Mexico things have a way of changing with elections. This
was even more true when Miguel Alemán was elected
president in 1946. For one thing, too, business wasn't too
good. All the big factories in San Diego closed after the
war and things sort of went back to normal. Then we had
trouble with bookmakers at the track; they were stealing
our action. All in all, our profits went down, but we were
still making a little money and staying in the black.

"Then one day, I think it was in August, 1947, I got
this telegram from Mexico City and it was signed by
Johnny Alessio. He's an American, an Italian from San
Diego, and he was the manager of Banco del Pacífico in
Tijuana. Well, the wire says: 'Don't sell to anyone until
you talk to me.' There was something else in there about
Alberto Aldrete (he was governor of Baja) also being
interested in buying the track and for me not to sell to
him until I had talked to Alessio. Anyhow, it was the first
news I had about the track being up for sale. One funny
thing was that a couple of months earlier I had barred
Alessio's brother, Russell, from the track for bookmaking.
So I went to Mexico City to talk to my backers and found

that Camacho and Quevedo had already sold out to
Alemán and a supreme court judge by the name of
Carranca. So Alessio offered eighty-five thousand dollars
for my stock and the gambling permit, which still had
about eight years to run, and I took it. The rest is history.
Mr. Alessio is still at the track, doing very well, I might
add. He's a multimillionaire and a very prominent citizen
on both sides of the line. Now, that's really the story you
ought to write; you know, from shoeshine boy to the top,
a real American classic."

As with all great contemporary American classics, it
begins with the labors of a press agent and The Profile:
"John S. Alessio was born of immigrant parents, Mr. and
Mrs. Dominic Alessio, in Clarksburg, W. Va., June 24,
1910. He is one of seven sons, the others being Frank,
Russell, Louis, Joseph, Angelo and Tony. The father, in
failing health, brought his family to San Diego, Calif., in
1920, and, because of the elder Alessio's condition, the
four oldest boys — Frank, John, Russell and Louis — had
to go to work at an early age. John attended school only
through the seventh grade and then obtained employment as a shoeshine boy in downtown San Diego. One of
his customers was C. Arnholt Smith, then associated with
the Bank of Italy and now one of San Diego's leading
financiers. When John lost his job because the building in
which his shoeshine stand was located was torn down to
make room for new construction, Smith told him of an
opening in the Banco del Pacífico, a bank in Tijuana,
Mexico. Shortly thereafter, Alessio became a messenger

for the Mexican bank. That was in 1929, and at the time John could not speak a word of Spanish. He grasped every opportunity to learn the language, with the result that today he has a complete command of it. At the bank he was promoted from messenger to teller, then took over the foreign exchange department, moved up to assistant manager and, in 1943, became manager. In 1947 he was offered an opportunity to identify himself with the Caliente Racetrack as its assistant general manager, and, from the time he accepted the assignment, he began the process of expanding and modernizing the plant, improving the caliber of racing and elevating the prestige of the operation. . . ."

At this point, The Profile skips to 1953, leaving out considerable history. For example, this story in the San Diego *Union* on October 15, 1947: "A sweeping shakeup of Banco del Pacífico executives was reported here today, as the parent Banco Nacional de México assertedly continued its examination of a 'heavy' loan made to Alberto V. Aldrete Sr., Governor of the Northern District of Baja California. Reports also persisted that Aldrete intends to resign the governorship, after a leave of absence. Although resignation of John Alessio as Manager of the Tijuana Banco del Pacífico branch was announced previously, it was not learned until today that five other key executives subsequently have been fired or have resigned, including Eloy Martínez, who manages the eight-branch banking chain. . . . The executive shakeup in the bank reportedly resulted from the loan, variously rumored to be from 25 to 55 million pesos (between five and 11 million U.S. dollars)."

A year later, October 12, 1948, the *Union* reported: "A third accusation involving misuse of funds of the Banco del Pacífico was presented today by Mexico City bank officials against Alberto Aldrete, Tecate brewer, and six suspended bank employes. This accusation, made in court here before Judge Gabriel Moreno Lozano, charged the defendants with fraud and breach of trust in the amount of $3,496,173.85 (U.S.) representing bank funds lent to Aldrete. The complaint charged that the Tijuana bank employes made it appear that the money was deposited in the U.S. National Bank [owned by C. Arnholt Smith] in San Diego. . . . Alessio appeared in court but refused to testify after the prosecuting attorney presented 39 documents as evidence against him and associates."

A *Union* story on June 10, 1949, pictures Alessio, who had been cleared of charges in Mexico, living in Tijuana as an American fugitive: "A San Francisco warrant for John Alessio, former manager of the Banco del Pacífico in Tijuana, for his arrest on grand theft and conspiracy charges, is still active in San Diego police files . . . [they] have been waiting for Alessio to come across the border to serve the warrant. Alessio was indicted last September by the San Francisco grand jury following an inquiry into a million-dollar loan obtained from Pacific Vegetable Oil Co. for transactions involving the Tecate Brewery."

Propped up in a huge leather chair behind an enormous desk in his racetrack office, John Alessio (a softly rounded

little man in a dark, slenderizing business suit — hardly
the Johnny O'Clock or Mr. Lucky type) sits stiffly among
the legions of celebrities and dignitaries surrounding him
— perplexed grins frozen by a busy flack, trapped recipi-
ents of vigorous handshakes and backslaps (often both
simultaneously), all familiar faces (from movie stars to
presidents) captured in perpetuity, prizes on display before a passing parade of impressed underlings. "Yes, it's
true," he says, dark eyes peering intently through horn-
rimmed magnifying lenses. "What happened here was
that many years ago a fellow by the name of Aldrete was
the owner of a brewery in Tecate and a cottonseed business in Mexicali. And the first thing you know, after he
became governor, he started demanding that everybody
buy his beer, and that they sell him their cotton. He had
a monopoly, and he started stepping on the toes of many
big customers. These customers went into Mexico City
and started a lot of political trouble. His son, Alberto, Jr.,
made some loans and they were discounted in San Francisco, on the assumption that they could pay them all
with cottonseed oil and beer, and all that. They felt that
it was misrepresentation; and I went to San Francisco one
time, as an interpreter, although Mr. Aldrete spoke perfect English. Our general manager, Mr. Eloy Martínez, in
Hermosillo, did not; and one afternoon they said that I
participated in a meeting in San Francisco where they had
secured some money with misrepresentation. So they
picked us up down here; of course, we were all well liked,
and were all acquitted, including myself. They were very

nice with me. I stayed with them, and many times I was told that I could go back to the States, but I said that I definitely would not leave without seeing it through.

"Then the masterpiece of all came. They felt that if I got out of this, they would charge me with this situation in San Francisco. And that turned out to be the most amusing one of all. That is when I first met Pat Brown [now one of Alessio's attorneys]. He was district attorney in San Francisco. Well, they had me registered in the Palace Hotel. That I had stayed there that afternoon or that night, because I was an interpreter. My little Irish wife, talking to me several days later, said, how could you be in San Francisco when you were with the two little girls and I over in, I think, in the northern part of the state, in the hills there, taking a couple days' vacation. So with that I went back and saw our attorney in San Francisco, and he walked in and said to Pat Brown, 'Pat, you've got something here that is not going to be good for you. Mr. Alessio was not even here.' Within seventy-two hours, they went before the judge and dismissed the charges."

Two men are credited with having saved Alessio from prison. Enrique Parra, envoy without portfolio in many of Miguel Alemán's financial involvements, interceded on Alessio's behalf with the Mexican police and courts. And it was Parra who stopped the extradition. In the United States, it was Don Keller, district attorney of San Diego for twenty-seven years, who came to his rescue, at the behest of Alessio's mentor, C. Arnholt Smith, who by

then had covered considerable mileage on that long road
to success. Aldrete, Jr., and Martínez were later kidnaped
and forced across the border at gun point; they were
indicted in San Francisco, tried, convicted, and released
on probation.

According to The Profile, Alessio "became the track's
executive director in 1953, the position he still holds and
which puts him in full authority insofar as the activities of
Caliente and its policies are concerned."

The question of ownership is one that props Alessio
even higher in his chair: "Gonzalo Gonzáles is still president of the company. And he is the one who came to see
me in 1947 and asked me if I would help him run the
racetrack. At that time I was Silveyra's assistant, interpreter and everything else. Things didn't go too well with
him, and they asked me to see if I couldn't find someone
to run this racetrack, and I got a fellow named Walter C.
Marty. I have been in Mexico for thirty-eight years. I was
called upon by Gonzalo and his group. I personally didn't
want to come here, but they told me it would be to my
advantage, being in Mexico. I said, 'Okay,' and that's how
I started in racing." You came in as manager? "No, no! I
came in as Mr. Marty's assistant. I was more or less, well,
I would still say I was his interpreter because I speak a
little Spanish. I took care of all the personal stuff for the
Mexico City people and all that." Mr. Parra was in this
group? "Well, as I say, I did all my contacts with Mr.
Gonzalo Gonzáles. I do know that there were influential
businessmen in this organization, which there still are

today." Who are these men? "I really wouldn't know, because, after all, the company is a Mexican corporation. We as American citizens can only apply ourselves to the laws here, which is exactly what I did. I still apply myself to the Mexican laws."

There is a law in Mexico that precludes a foreigner from owning land within a hundred kilometers of the frontier or seacoast. Tijuana Mayor Francisco "Pancho" López Gutiérrez is convinced that Alessio is more than executive director at Caliente: "Yes, he owns the land. Well, more precisely, Hipodromo de Tijuana owns it and he has title to the company. He might deny it because he is an American citizen, but he owns it."

As to the Juárez racetrack, The Profile offers this explanation: "With a group of associates, Alessio built the multimillion-dollar Juárez Race Track in Juárez, Mexico, just across the international border from El Paso, Texas, and when its doors opened in May of 1964 sports writers immediately tagged it with the glamorous title of 'Taj Mahal of Racing.' "

Alessio: "From time to time, we have people come in and look over our operation here. They are usually a little intrigued with it, 'cause it's the only track that has horses and dogs within the one complex. So we get opportunities to meet people that are interested in us going into their areas. For instance, in Juárez, the biggest breeder (there's his picture on that wall), Mr. Hernández, and there's Mr. Antonio Bermúdez of PEMEX, director of PRONAF — the border beautification program. They invited me to come down and build this type of complex there, and I said yes. So I went down there and built it for *them*." You don't own it? "I don't own anything. The only thing that I can tell you is that I am an American citizen, and I have promoted myself up the line and stayed in good character. Call it salary, call it bonuses, and all that."

Juárez attorney González Vargas looks at the racetrack with suspicion: "They don't pay a penny's tax to the city or state. They got a tax exemption on the strength that it was an industry beneficial to the city and state. What industry? I don't understand industry that way. What does it produce? Yes, everybody knows that Alemán is the man behind Alessio. But it works both ways. A lot of Alessio's investments in San Diego and Beverly Hills — there's a whole block on Wilshire — involve Alemán money."

"How Alessio got to open the track in Juárez after many, many turndowns of other promoters, I don't know," says reporter Marshall Hail. "Those Alessio boys intrigue me. I wish I knew more about them. I think some people confuse Alessio with a gangster by the same name who got bumped off a couple of years ago in New York. I know a lot of people around here were saying that a gangster built the Juárez track. I do know that Pete Muñoz — he's a fugitive from an arms-smuggling case here in the States — got the concession from Alessio to provide feed for the horses and dogs at the track."

Once when arriving in Juárez, Alessio discovered that a sealed envelope containing currency was missing. He

phoned the Los Angeles police and asked them to check
the plane he had transferred from in Los Angeles. When
they called to say they had found it, he thanked them and
said it would be taken care of. Moments later, one of
Mayor Sam Yorty's administrative assistants picked it up
and took the next flight to El Paso, personally delivering
the envelope to Alessio.

"On paper," one government agent observed, "Alessio
is an employee of about eighteen Mexican corporations in
Tijuana alone. Of course, in reality he owns these companies in the names of third parties, mostly low category–
type employees and relatives. We interviewed several of
these employees, and the story we get is consistent with
this type of operation. For example, one such employee
was carried on paper as an official of one of these corporations at a salary of 5,000 pesos a month. Every month he
was presented with a check for this amount, which he
would endorse and hand right back to Alessio's secretary.
However, the primary function of these corporations is to
facilitate the flight of money from Mexico into this country, legalizing it in the process. A case in point was the sale
of racing equipment by International Leasing Corporation, a subsidiary of the Alessio Corporation, to Inversiones de Baja California, a Mexican corporation owned
by Alessio. Salvadore Lemus, an employee of the track,
signed as secretary, and Angelo Serena (he runs a restaurant in Tijuana) as president of Inversiones. Angelo
Alessio signed as president of International Leasing,
which in this transaction received $800,000 for the sale of

equipment which was already owned by Caliente and was worth only a small fraction of the amount involved. This is one way Alessio gets American dollars into California from Mexican investments. Another of Alessio's dummy corporations, Tusa, S.A. [S.A. means Society Anonymous; it protects the identity of the incorporators] owned a yacht, *Salado,* anchored at Alessio's Kona Kai Club in San Diego. Caliente paid the Kona Kai $1,000 a month to lease the *Salado,* plus an average of $9,000 monthly for its membership. Caliente buys just about everything from other Alessio corporations. For example, Champ Advertising (Alessio's) receives about a half-million a year from Caliente. International Leasing was paid $10,929.85 for sign rentals for which it paid $3,730.52 to Charles Pepitone, whose associations in San Diego have included Mafia types. Alessio's Giovanni ranch in Tecate is owned by a Mexican corporation." (Alessio: "No, no! I don't own no ranch.") "These are just a few examples. It involves millions upon millions, and most of it coming from the gambling operation, which is unquestionably the largest bookmaking apparatus in the western hemisphere, if not the world."

Caliente offers two types of year-round racing: greyhounds on five nights (Wednesday through Sunday), and horses on two afternoons (Saturday and Sunday). The weekend mutuel handle ranges close to a million. While tracks in California are allowed to keep 14 percent (5 percent to the state and 9 percent to the track) of the handle, Caliente starts at a base of 24 percent on the win pools and 28 percent on the show pools. Although it is legal in Mexico, experienced horse players know that it makes the odds against them unbeatable.

The most popular form of mutuel gambling is the Five-Ten, a type of betting pool imported from Venezuela by Alessio in 1957, and similar to the twin doubles at Eastern tracks. Strictly a longshot player's dream, the Five-Ten requires successful handicapping of the fifth through tenth races. The pools have soared as high as $140,000, with 75 percent of it going to the players selecting the most winners, and 25 percent to the ones picking the second greatest number. The track, according to its program, takes only a 10 percent commission off the top. However, a little basic arithmetic placed the commission at 24.1 percent, a fact Alessio acknowledged only after he was confronted with the figures.

Alessio: "You looked probably at a publication that we had when we first came out with the Five-Ten." It's the one currently offered. "Well, still you go to a hotel room and find some kind of an ad that the hotel has there about a free sightseeing trip and you go there and they charge you for it. Our commission here in all our types of betting is 20 percent. Out of that 20 percent, we have to give the federal government approximately 5 percent [precisely 4 percent] and another 3 percent between the state and city [the governor and mayor are presently unaware of this bonanza]. So we are working with maybe about a net of 12 percent." You say it's 20 percent for the Five-Ten? "Yes, it's all the same." The difference yesterday between the handle and winnings amounted to 24.1 percent. "That's true. One and a half years ago, upon taking office, Mr. Díaz Ordaz (here I'm shaking hands with him) inherited the Olympics and the Congress passed a bill. Now, we, as management, fought it. And it says, until the Olympics are prepared, any type of sports activities involving betting must charge 4 percent to the public to finance the Olympics. So you find at the present time, from all winning tickets, a 4 percent charge; 4 percent and a fraction, exactly."

"I've seen a horse break out from the gate, get out in front, and be five or six lengths ahead coming around the turn into the stretch, and you'd just know he was going to win. Maybe he'd be ten to one, and I'd watch that tote board while everybody is watching the race. But me, I'm down there to watch that tote board, and at the same time I've got my camera there taking pictures, and I've seen the odds drop like say from seven to two. Just one number changed, that's all. There was no corresponding increase in the handle. Snap, just like that. I'd sure like to know how it's done" — from the recollections of a disciplined bettor.

Alessio: "Oh, hell, listen, in this kind of business, it's the greatest. The fellow that does the betting is the most disciplined individual. We've had people actually take pictures of our tote board outside, and go home and figure the mutuel. They don't understand that at the beginning there is always what we call breakage, just a fraction, and we explain it to them, of course."

Of all the ways of gambling at Caliente, and there are many, the Five-Ten is one of the most attractive to investigators. The form used in the Five-Ten consists of an original that is kept by the track and a duplicate given to the player. It enumerates six races, the fifth through the tenth, and for two dollars the player is allowed to select one horse in each of the six races. Or the player may write a multiple ticket, called a wheel, and select as many horses as he wishes, but it will cost him. For instance, if he picked four horses in each race, the ticket would run over eight thousand dollars. The rules, as promulgated by Caliente, stipulate that a "single" winner must consent to being photographed for publicity purposes. This proviso does not include multiple winners, who are paid in cash, unknown to the public.

An unusual insight into the Five-Ten operation was provided by a Caliente employee: "In other words, one winner gets a check, big fanfare and his picture in the track's gallery. The next week the newspapers report that fifteen people selected five horses, the most winners picked that day. One of them was John Smith, but the other fourteen remained anonymous. The joke around the track is 'Well, here goes Alessio again.' Since the inception of the Five-Ten in 1957, there have been over a thousand pools and all you see in the gallery are the pictures of about forty single winners, and all were milked for every ounce of publicity the track could squeeze out of them. Sometimes even bona fide winners get a fast shuffle. The Five-Ten form specifies that the validity of the ticket is to be judged solely by the track. Some winners, who were refused payment for one reason or another, have filed suit in the civil courts in Mexico, but their cases are dormant and will remain so until the second coming of Jesus.

"This brings to mind the famous 'kidnaping' (that's with quotes) case of Tony Alessio. It is, by the way, the case history presented to tourists visiting the FBI building in Washington. But our version around here is a little bit different. It all started with a Mr. X presenting a properly validated Five-Ten ticket that showed he was the sole winner of the pool, but the track couldn't find the original. So here was a very serious dilemma. It proved that persons inside the track could validate tickets at will. Now the track had two courses: turn Mr. X over to the Mexican federal authorities and prosecute him for fraud, or refuse payment and at worst fight it out in the civil courts. The track lawyers said that under no circumstances could they release this ticket back to Mr. X, or to anyone else, because it was prima facie evidence of accessibility to a machine. They decided to give Mr. X a receipt, but very carefully avoided the word fraud, because if there's one thing they don't want it's to bring in any outside investigative force that might want to look over the operation. So they decided to use the word irregular. Mr. X's fatal mistake was in surrendering the ticket. It then developed that Mr. X had four partners, and that the five of them had pooled their money to purchase a stamped blank ticket from a cashier. This cashier said (I'm quoting hearsay at the track): 'You gave me five thousand dollars and if you've got the guts to insist on payment, you'll get paid because the ticket is valid. Just leave me out of it.' Mr. X and his partners got themselves a Mexican lawyer, a very bad shyster, and filed a civil action. When this hit the newspapers, the track's legal department immediately replied that the ticket was irregular and that the pool had already been paid out to two other winners, who remained anonymous, and never existed as far as anybody knew. But to the public, the track had met its commitment and salvaged its reputation for honesty and fair play.

"Mr. X's attorney was called to Caliente and escorted into Mr. Alessio's office. Here's the gist of what transpired, as reported by one of the secretaries. Alessio: 'Mr. Attorney, I understand you are representing the interests of Mr. X, who has a ticket that was, as far as I'm concerned, fraudulently obtained here at the track. And, as you know, I'm just a small cog in a big wheel. I'm here to protect the interests of the public and the interests of men higher up in government, and I know that you want to get ahead in your career and also that you live off of your profession as a lawyer. I have a great deal of respect for you, a great deal of admiration. I've never called you in before because I've been so busy. I like you and I want to reaffirm our friendship. How much are you going to make out of this ticket?' 'Well,' he says, 'I have a percentage.' 'Look,' says Alessio, 'if you continue with this case, you know you're going to lose it. Not only that, but it's going to hurt you.' Alessio then reached into a drawer and

brought out a stack of bills which he pushed across the
desk to the lawyer. 'Don't misinterpret this gift,' he said.
'It's of my own free will. I'm giving it to you because I
don't want to see you get hurt. And I would advise you to
let Mr. X know that due process of the law is being followed here in Mexico and that severe action will be taken
against him.' Mr. X was promptly advised by his attorney
to haul his ass right out of the country because things
were going very wrong. He later signed a statement releas-
ing his interest in the ticket. But before this came to pass,
Mr. X had managed to interest the San Diego police in
his problem. This came about when the so-called *irregular*
ticket turned out to be *altered* when it was received by the
Mexican court. Now anybody with any sense knew that if
the ticket had been originally altered, Mr. X would have
found himself in the Tijuana jail, not the civil court. So
the San Diego police sent an officer to Tijuana to check
the court files. This immediately became known to Alessio,
who angrily summoned the officer to his office. I was a
witness to this encounter. The usual pat on the back was
administered with the usual reassurance that he wanted to
be the officer's friend, but that he had no business coming
into Tijuana and much less going into a case that was
before the courts of Mexico, in respect to a ticket that was
none of his business. Still, he was very much interested in
the officer's career and he wanted him to know that he,
himself, was only a little man representing powerful
forces, and that these powerful forces were so powerful he
just had to protect their interests and the interests of the

public. And 'By God, Mr. So-and-So, I want to be your friend, I want to shake your hand.' The officer acted like a true policeman. He said, 'I, too, am a little man in a big operation. I came here following orders, and I shall continue to obey the orders of my superiors.' 'Well, don't take it wrong. I just wanted you to know the ticket is in the proper hands.'

"Mr. X's partners were not as easily intimidated. They saw Harry Rosen, the manager of the Five-Ten, and offered to settle for the five thousand dollars they had invested in the ticket. Rosen flatly refused and they went to Tony Alessio, and the new leader of this group said, 'Tony, this ticket is worth seventy thousand dollars; I'll take anything. Give me half. You know me, I've been a client of this track for many years, and you know I wouldn't do anything wrong. I just want what's due me.' I will now repeat a rumor of the inner circle to the effect that at this time John and Tony were not on speaking terms because of the heavy gambling losses incurred by Tony in Las Vegas and other places. Well, Mr. X's four partners cooked up the kidnaping of Tony, and from beginning to end, a Boy Scout could have solved the case. Mr. Alessio, always the businessman, brought down the reward from $600,000 to $200,000 for Tony's life, which caused additional family strain. Tony was held in a small hotel, with thin walls separating the rooms, and kept there a couple days with only a girl to guard him. She even went out for sandwiches. Rank amateurs. These guys were so naïve they were visually tracked. They telephoned the girl to release Tony the moment they got the money, instead of waiting to get out of the area, and they were captured by the FBI. They were convicted, and their story to this day is that Tony was in on it, a charge many people at the track would like to believe.

"John Alessio is sitting on top of a very volatile situation, politics being what they are in Mexico. Considering the millions involved, with no records as such to present before any court, the problem was pretty much solved when, in an attempt to improve the track, a concrete encasement was built over the Five-Ten office (the whole place is a firetrap) to house all the files. Not long after its completion, a fire broke out inside the encasement, consuming all the records. The Tijuana papers, which are very partial to Alessio, praised the track for having confined the fire to the encasement. Hell, we couldn't even get water in there — there was no water at all."

Benjamin García, the treasurer at Caliente (he first worked for Alessio as a teller at Banco del Pacífico), has accumulated substantial real estate (including the BIC and Serena restaurants in Tijuana) and other wealth in the past twenty years — he has reportedly won the Five-Ten at least five times against pretty steep odds. Recently, he received a $250,000 unsecured loan from Southland Finance, another Alessio corporation, and the note was later bought by Charles Pepitone.

Alessio: "No, you can't talk to Benny García. He's got orders not to divulge any information; we don't like to give out publicity. And many times he has been closemouthed there. He handles thousands and thousands of dollars, the whole bankroll there. So you hear all kinds of stories. About the only thing Benny García has done in his life is work hard and accumulate some real status in this town. Anybody who had any vision here, they could accumulate a little money and buy real estate years ago. Today he is reaping the profits, because property went sky high. Just like anyplace else." Has he won the Five-Ten? "These individuals around here, even this little girl walking out of here right now, they all take a Five-Ten pool. They might of won, but never won a big one."

The most lucrative operation at Caliente is the Foreign Book, managed by Russell Alessio, which accepts wagers on horse races run all over the North American continent. It is a legal bookmaking operation, subject to the same controls a bookmaker would establish on odds — no longshots. U.S. federal agents estimate the weekly net at fifteen thousand dollars. They also have linked Caliente to Las Vegas, with layoff action flowing both ways (this resulted in Russell Alessio's conviction for bookmaking in 1968 — details later in this chapter).

A supplement to this operation is the Future Book, which accepts wagers on potential or specific entries in high-stake races like the Santa Anita Handicap and the Kentucky Derby. Odds on potential entries may run as high as 1,000 to 1, months before the event, with the proviso that if the horse is scratched, the track keeps the wager. In the event Caliente becomes heavily committed to a potential winner, the practice is to send a confidant to the track on the day of the race to feed a percentage of the handle into the mutuel, not only to cover themselves, but to lower the odds.

Alessio: "As far as the Foreign Book is concerned, you'd be surprised at the number of retired people living around Coronado and La Mesa and Oceanside who come down here and just make it their day's work. That's what they live for. They even bring cakes and pies: little old ladies and old boys. Now, as far as bookmaking is concerned, we could tell every bookmaker in the country to call in here — we'll take your bets and all that. We have discouraged it. Our concession will not allow us to take a bet over the phone or by mail. So we rely on the people who come here, the tourists or the little retired ones who make it their business, or the Mexican people — well, little by little they are getting around to it." Do you net 30 percent? "One of the greatest pricemakers in the business was Walter C. Marty, and he was my teacher. To quote him, he used to tell me, 'John, anytime you're running a book and you are not keeping 12 to 14 percent, something is wrong with your book. Either somebody is stealing or they're writing tickets after the races are run. But if you take 30 percent, you won't have any customers left. You'll just grind them out.' As to the Future Book, we use it mainly as a form of advertising. We get our odds on the AP and UPI wire and consequently in the nation's press. But there's no money in it."

In the summer of 1958, Governor Braulio Maldonado, reaching the end of his six-year term, permitted casino gambling to return to Baja California, this time in the little resort community of Rosarito Beach, fifteen miles south of Tijuana.

"The governor's cousin got seventy-five thousand dollars to let them start this gambling club," says José Gorduno, publisher of Tijuana's *Las Noticias*. "This was the hush money. Then they went ahead and formed the Club Deportivo Panamericano, S.A. It was headed by Eddie Nealis, who ran the racetrack here during the war, and John Alessio. Governor Maldonado made speeches in California about the gambling, saying there was nothing illegal, that they were only playing the games allowed by Mexican law, which was an outright lie. The only betting permitted in Mexico is on horse and dog racing, jai alai and the lottery."

René Monteverde, touted as the Toots Shor of Tijuana when he owned the Coronet restaurant (this was before his conviction in a U.S. court for selling narcotics to a federal agent — Walter Winchell was a character witness at his trial), says it was common knowledge in Tijuana that John Alessio was a partner of Nealis, along with Michel Marchese, a New York narcotics trafficker. ("You should have seen Marchese's Dun & Bradstreet report," says a Los Angeles police official. "It was beautiful. He had ranches, mining properties, oil wells, and the sonofabitch, before he was knocked over on a big narco deal [sentence, one to ten years] and became a snitch for one of the federal agencies, was nothing but a goddamn barber and gangster, and that's all he was.")

"Jesus, but they had a great setup over there," says

Monteverde, jumping from his chair to pace the room, pacing obviously being his favorite memory-priming device, and no doubt a conditioned reflex from the old days when he paced among the tables of his *boite*, the reigning panjandrum of Tijuanian haute society. "They redecorated the old Rosarito Beach hotel and converted a beautiful home next to it into a plush casino. They got a high-caliber mailing list and sent out membership cards all over Southern California, stating that policemen guards were there for their protection. Well, Jesus, they came by the hundreds and the thousands. Eddie told me not long after they opened up that by the next summer the place wasn't going to be big enough, business was so good. But they were always scared; at the end especially when they knew that something had gone wrong. Of course, they were getting heat from Johnny Rosselli, the Mafia boss in Las Vegas, because a lot of hardcore gamblers switched to Rosarito. It's only a hundred and twenty-eight miles from L.A. to the border, and hardcore gamblers don't care for the Vegas hassle; you know, the glamor bit, the crowds, the fighting for a seat at a blackjack table, or the bar, and the whores everywhere. They've got a thousand or a hundred bucks, and it's win or lose; boom, I'm finished, that's my two hours. Why fly to Vegas? Rosarito was a lot closer. So, you know, the Rosarito bit was sort of living on borrowed time."

The Las Vegas heat was directed at John Alessio. A few days after Alessio sold his interest to Nealis, soldiers and federal police came in from Mexico City and closed the casino.

In response to a question about his partnership with Nealis, Alessio offered this explanation: "I'm going to give you the story on that. I was even out of town when it was raided. We had a governor here, who apparently gave Eddie the okay to open it up, but conservative. And I was out of town when they first went in and told him to close up. Eddie told me that as long as he had the go-ahead from the governor, he didn't have to close up. I was so perturbed, so many of the people picked up in the raid were such undesirables. They found a couple of stolen cars and all that."

The raid, planned for a Saturday, did not come until late Sunday afternoon (January 25, 1959) — the airplane carrying police and soldiers was detoured to Mexicali because of a heavy fog. To avoid any leak of the impending raid, they slept on the plane that night. Sixty-three Americans were caught in the raid and lodged in the Tijuana jail. Nealis, who operated the casino for six months, managed to escape. "When they took the soldiers from the beach front to eat breakfast," he says, "I just took a hike up the beach to San Diego."

Alessio: "I've built ten schools in Tijuana and one in Tecate. One is named after my father, another after President Kennedy, and the rest after great Mexican heroes and leaders." With your own money? "No, the racetrack corporation's." You were able to persuade the owners to sponsor this charity? "I've been able to do a lot of things."

In an age of public relations, "image" is the name of

the game. A second Caliente employee elaborates on this subject: "A few years ago a program was cooked up to create a new image of Mr. Alessio. The idea was to present him as a great philanthropist and political power. It involved two programs: schools would be built, and donations made to the poor at Christmas. All of this was carefully preconceived and elaborated. And, surprisingly enough, conceived in a manner that it would not cost Mr. Alessio one cent, and he would profit financially from this image projected internationally. The image buildup was very easy with the free access he has to the press in Tijuana and San Diego. As to the schools, a plot of land was acquired free from government-owned land or donated outright by some humble person apprised of this great program for the children of Tijuana. Once the plot was acquired, the cornerstone was laid, and he always made it a point that all news media, including radio and television, were present and took due note. Once this cornerstone was laid, his image as a philanthropist received widespread notice, and contributions were made directly to Mr. Alessio; one contributor being Mr. Roscoe Hazard, the San Diego contractor, a good man in my opinion, who had no knowledge of the situation. The school would be built with cheap labor, mostly out of cheap materials.

"In Mexico, federal law stipulates that the raising of the flag, at the inauguration of any public building, will be done by the military. Taking advantage of this situation, Mr. Alessio would see to it that a choice group of soldiers were sent to the school on inauguration day, and, of course, leading American authorities in the area would attend, including, if at all possible, the governors on both sides of the line. Once everyone was seated, Mr. Alessio in the front row with all the dignitaries, and the Mexican commanding general of the area present, in full regalia, and the military lined up with the drum and bugle corps, and the general standing at attention, Mr. Alessio would approach the general at a distance away from the reviewing stand and mention some simple phrase of gratitude, 'Good morning, General; how are you feeling? We are at your orders; anytime you wish to commence the flag-raising ceremonies, please do so.' The general would, of course, salute, and Mr. Alessio would convey the impression that he was giving orders to the general. The general would wheel around and order a captain to play the necessary music for the flag-raising ceremony. Well, the governor was thanked for his co-operation and the master of ceremonies, who was Mr. Alessio's public relations director, would make the official presentation of all the high-ranking government officials surrounding Mr. Alessio. Now, do you get the picture? The school cost him, I would estimate, the equivalent of seven thousand dollars; it would be ballooned to fifty thousand dollars for tax-deduction purposes."

Did Alessio boast of his political connections in California? "Often. He was a great admirer of Governor Brown and a great partisan of his. He was very proud of the fact they were on a first-name basis. He contributed to the Democratic party on a continuing basis, and said once that he had given Mr. Brown fifty thousand dollars. But he's so egotistical we took his statements with a grain of salt — knowing of his connections in Mexico and how phony these so-called legal transactions were, you see. I do know one time he was very disturbed and hurt because he didn't receive an official invitation from Brown to attend a presidential inauguration. He was not stupid enough to complain about it, but in his diplomatic inference that he had not received it, he morally obligated Brown to send the invitation. In other words, he did ultimately get the invitation, and I understand he did fly with Brown to Washington, and he did have credential entry into the Senate area as a guest."

Alessio's enchantment with the Democratic party lasted until Brown's gubernatorial defeat in 1966. Two years later, Alessio contributed (with his family) twenty thousand dollars to Nixon's campaign, and was once again a privileged guest at the inauguration.

Skipping over voluminous highlights in The Profile, this item catches the eye: "In April, 1960, in company with his brothers Angelo, Russell and Tony, he acquired the historic Hotel Del Coronado. Regarded among the world's great resort centers, the hotel, occupying 17 land-scaped acres, represented an initial investment of approximately $2,500,000, and in the months following its purchase the Alessio Corporation expended upwards of another million dollars in a tremendous restoration program.

In the summer of 1963 Alessio sold the [hotel] and 20 acres of adjacent beach frontage along Coronado's Silver Strand for a reported price in excess of $7,000,000. Soon thereafter, Alessio announced the acquisition of the private Kona Kai Club and the adjoining public Kona Inn on San Diego's Shelter Island. At the same time he announced preliminary plans for construction of an 800-room high-rise convention hotel near San Diego's new Center City complex. This was to be a joint venture between the Alessio Corporation and the Westgate-California Corporation headed by C. Arnholt Smith, San Diego banker and industrialist — the same C. Arnholt Smith who many years earlier had been instrumental in helping Alessio get his start in the banking business. At the same time he broke ground on a handsome 12-story office building covering an entire city block on heights overlooking San Diego's business district. Known as the Fifth Avenue Financial Centre, it towers 426 feet above San Diego bay, and dignitaries from throughout California, headed by Gov. Edmund G. Brown, attended dedication ceremonies in July, 1965."

At last, the Horatio Alger climax: the monolithic merger of patron and protégé. Alessio: "What we did, we had a little real-estate company, we had bought up some property, what we call naked property, no buildings on it, and all that. So, from there we went over into San Diego and extensified our real-estate holdings a little more as we went along. Then one afternoon we decided that we would merge part of our assets with Westgate. In other words, when you buy property today you buy it on paper and all that. All our paper was converted over into West-gate-California Corporation, as far as some of our real estate — I would say maybe 80 percent of our assets was merged. That is how we became connected with West-gate. Of course, I've known Mr. Alessio [sic] — I've known Mr. Smith these many years. He's had a very fine success." Conjugally, this is true: Alessio, the versatile Democrat, and Smith, the staunch Republican, *do* enjoy a very fine success, indeed. The conjugated force of Westgate-California brought together an impressive collection of some fifty subsidiaries, operating in a broad spectrum of industries and services in six states (California, Nevada, Arizona, Oregon, Missouri, and Delaware) and Mexico — excluding, of course, Hipodromo de Tijuana, the Juárez racetrack, the Mexicali Foreign Book, and other Mexican entities "managed" by Alessio or dummy companies in the names of third parties.

Besides the U.S. National Bank (44 branches with assets of $494.6 million at the end of 1968), Smith-Alessio moves in such diverse economic circles as truck fleets, cargo hauling and truck leasing; taxi fleets (Yellow Cab companies in San Francisco, Oakland, Daly City and Los Angeles International Airport); advertising and public relations; tuna fishing (twelve vessels); food canning (Breast-O-Chicken and Carnation seafood, Gifford's & Girard's olives, Girard's salad dressing and related products); electronics; finance and fund management; hotels, office buildings, shopping centers; real estate and land

development; rentals, leases and subleases; high-rise and
other ·construction; insurance and re-insurance; baseball
(San Diego Padres, a new entry in the National League);
dog racing (Yuma and Caliente greyhound clubs); plus a
continuing program of growth: borrow, loan, merge, di-
vide, multiply, keep growing — buy, buy, buy; why not?
"It's only paper, and all that."

A long piece in the *Wall Street Journal* on April 16,
1969, labeled Smith a "self-dealing tycoon" and went on
to detail "how a Californian uses publicly owned firms to
aid private ventures."

In its investigation, the *Journal* turned up "scores of
deals in which private concerns controlled by Mr. Smith
or related individuals have made large and sometimes
quick profits on sales of land, small firms and securities to
Westgate-California, which has about 8,600 stockholders.
Westgate-California has let contracts to companies in
which associates of Mr. Smith had interests, and at least
two Smith-related private companies continue to enjoy an
unusual and profitable relationship with Westgate-California. U.S. National Bank has provided the financing for
a number of these transactions. It has 3,700 shareholders.
Meantime, the earnings performance of Mr. Smith's publicly owned firms has been less than spectacular."

One of the many deals detailed in the story involved
two privately owned companies, Westgate-California
Products, Inc., whose president and principal stockholder
is C. Arnholt's brother, John Smith; and J. R. Barry Co.,
owned by J. R. Barry, who is marketing vice-president of

Westgate-California Foods, Inc., a Westgate-California subsidiary, and by John Alessio. "The usual way that U.S. tuna processors get their product in the hands of retailers is through middlemen called food brokers," said the *Journal*, "who receive commissions ranging from 2% to 4% of the wholesale price. Beginning in January 1966, however, Westgate-California inserted Westgate-California Products and J. R. Barry between itself and the brokers, cutting in the private firms for additional commissions . . . [totaling] . . . $633,500 in 1966 and $825,000 in 1967."

"Jesus, that article was a shot in the arm to the community," a TV executive told me. "Imagine, a newspaper three thousand miles away telling us about the financial hanky-pankies of one of our merchant princes."

Shortly after Nixon's election, there were rumors in San Diego that Smith was a strong contender for Navy Secretary. Just in August, 1968, the San Diego *Union* had triumphantly recounted Smith's coup in Miami: "Richard and Pat Nixon shook maybe 5,000 hands yesterday at a delegates' reception, but the first two hands they shook belonged to San Diegans. They are Mr. and Mrs. C. Arnholt Smith. Smith, a delegate to the Republican convention, received hearty handshakes, but Mrs. Smith received a kiss from each of the Nixons. What did the Smiths and the Nixons talk about in the receiving line? 'They were telling us,' said petite, raven-haired Mrs. Smith, 'that we would be their first guests in the White House.' The Smiths and the Nixons had planned to meet July 21 in Los Angeles, Mrs. Smith explained, but the

Smiths couldn't keep the date. They were being married that day. 'So,' she said, 'we thought we'd be the first ones here today.'" The *Union* neglected to report that Smith was in the small group that sweated out election night returns with Nixon in a New York hotel suite.

Alessio's "image" preoccupation is never far from the surface. "I was 'Man of the Year in Racing' in 1957," he says, without prompting, "and the presentation by the Jockey Guild of America was made at the Waldorf-Astoria in New York. Just recently the Exchange Club here in San Diego awarded me the Book of Golden Deeds, and in 1966 the University of San Diego awarded me an honorary Doctorate of Laws degree. Oh, I've been Mr. San Diego, Mr. Tijuana, Mr. Coronado, so many, it's hard to remember them all, but it makes me feel very, very humble and proud to receive all these recognitions; besides would I receive these fine awards if I didn't deserve them?" (C. Arnholt Smith was dubbed "Mr. San Diego of the Century," which is pretty hard to beat.)

James S. Copley's San Diego *Union* and *Evening Tribune* devote unlimited space to Alessio's words and deeds. For a typical sample of the slant, here are a few sentences from a feature story in the March 12, 1968, *Evening Tribune*: "In toto, Alessio is a driving ambitious tycoon of the first magnitude in San Diego industry and a sort of father-saint to Mexican children. . . . Alessio admits to a compulsion to help Mexicans — from the Caliente Christmas party to massive donations of equipment and money to the Red Cross of Mexico. . . . Besides his racing interests and his charity work south of the border, Alessio holds great fondness for Mexico. It is where he got his start."

"To watch John operate," says a Caliente employee, "is like watching the late-late show. He's accomplished all these things, fantastic wealth and political power in two countries, but socially he's nowhere, and it kills him. That's why he bought the Hotel Del Coronado and gave all those fancy parties. Oh, the social register came, but, as interpreted by him, they just didn't kow-tow to his aspirations, at least, not to his satisfaction. John lacks couth; he has a tough time mixing on any level higher than showbiz. It's a pretty sad picture: Mr. Coronado, the black and white ball, the people in their elegant dress, and there's John, sitting up there: 'Hey, Louie, com'ere. Git dem guys out of here.' And he's quick-tempered and so easily offended. Incredibly thin-skinned. And don't think it hasn't hurt his ego to know that Caliente is considered second-rate by international racing standards."

Alessio: "This is the granddaddy of all racing: the old Tijuana racetrack and Caliente, before there was even racing in California. Our purses are not too high, but let's say you have horses that are running in Santa Anita, they are running for ten thousand dollars — there is always the little horse that has gone into those races that starts going bad. So, they've got to find a place to run these horses, and the owners send them down here. All the top stables come down here and get stall space. They bring their yearlings in, that's the little babies, and they break them in as two-year-olds, and many of our horses, broken in down here, have gone out to make great records. Recently, I had an invitation from the governor of Nevada, through a group of businessmen and breeders in Reno. I went up there and he is a very fine, a *very* fine man. We visited and he said, 'Mr. Alessio, our racing here, we would like to expand it more.' The least I could do was suggest; I got his ideas and came back and went with my executive board and we set up a program." He picks up a huge stack of papers, and, with a weighing motion, graphically conveys the enormity of the project solved. "And I personally delivered it to him. It was a broad, bold report of what I thought we could do in Reno. And when I was there, naturally, it came out in the newspapers. The first thing you know, Mr. J. Kell Houssels, he's the owner of the Tropicana in Las Vegas, a very, *very* fine man [Alessio's emphasis on the good character of Nevadans may have been due to my having been the co-author of *The Green Felt Jungle* about Las Vegas gambling] telephoned me and said, 'Johnny, I would like to talk to you.' Mr. Houssels is chairman of the Nevada Racing Commission, and they passed a resolution and sent it to me saying that anything I want, they would be most pleased to work it out with us, for they want to revive racing on a higher standard. Racing failed in Las Vegas because they tried to upgrade it too much. They put this beautiful racetrack in Las Vegas and they brought in the finest stables, they spent money like it was going out of circulation. And they didn't have the backing of the little breeders in that state.

If they would've stayed within the standard of racing there, I think they would've been more successful. The same thing applies right here in Tijuana. If you look at our racing program today, we have, I wouldn't say, horses that are not fit to run — the stables in California have two or three kinds of horses, and we have maybe the second- or third-grade horses here — they are competitive in the racing, and they are still thoroughbreds."

Alessio's most ferocious headlong charge at the patrician gates of San Diego came in 1966 — it nearly proved the Götterdämmerung of his image. It began with his bid to acquire Del Mar, Bing Crosby's old "Where the Turf Meets the Surf" racetrack a few miles north of San Diego.

Alessio: "In the thirty-eight years that I've been in Mexico, I've always found that it is much nicer to serve than to receive. Because you can serve easy, but it's so hard to find people to serve you. You don't receive it that easy. In my life, I've worked hard and what do I find? You know, sometimes it makes me scratch my head. Some time ago I decided to form a group of people in San Diego because I'm community-minded there, and we decided that we were going to bid on the Del Mar Turf Club. Prior to that I had the most beautiful relations with the Hollywood and Santa Anita racetracks, with all the tracks. Right this afternoon, we had one of the commissioners from the state of New York here visiting. I've met them all. And at the moment, I wanted to become interested because this fine group of San Diego people wanted to keep it in the San Diego area, because the racetrack has always been run by people outside the state. Then my problems start. I don't know why. I'm sure I would conduct myself properly up there. We would run a good racetrack."

Alessio's "fine group of San Diego people" was formed into a loose partnership called Del Mar Associates (later incorporated) and among others it included his brother Angelo; his son-in-law's father, Manuel Rosa, a tuna-boat owner; Mrs. Carol Shannon, daughter of C. Arnholt Smith; Helen Álvarez Hill, now Mrs. C. Arnholt Smith; Harold S. Jurgensen, a stockholder and a member of the board of directors of the U.S. National Bank; Deputy Police Chief Blucher; and pawnshop operator Sammy Addleson. (Known as the Unslung Mayor of Fourth and F streets, and the Third Police Chief, Addleson testified before a 1968 grand jury investigating corruption in San Diego that he had collected "protection" money in the old days for the vice squad and the tax assessor's office.)

Harold Keen, a local television news commentator, was one of the first to visit "problems" on Alessio and his "fine group." "Alessio has been one of my most devoted enemies," says Keen. "That's because I'm one of the few who won't fall on his knees and praise Allah whenever he appears on the scene. When he tried to walk away in a very blatant manner with this Del Mar lease, even though his bid was only the second highest, we blasted the whole transaction pretty hard on television. The newspapers just went along because Alessio and Jim Copley have been somewhat associated through the years, and, of course, Smith and Copley are very close."

When the repercussions became statewide, Attorney

General Thomas C. Lynch launched an investigation into
the leasing procedure employed by the Board of Directors
of the Twenty-second Agriculture District, the landlord of
the state-owned racetrack. The A.G.'s report, submitted
on July 25, 1967, is particularly interesting when viewed
in the context of Alessio's "I'm sure I would conduct
myself properly up there."

The report's first conclusion ("The business connections and personal associations of Mr. Lewis Lipton, a
Board member, viewed in relation to his actions upon the
Del Mar lease, reveal a possible conflict of interest")
appears somewhat conservative in the light of Lipton's
position as a vice-president of the U.S. National Bank.

Lipton described his initial employment by C. Arnholt
Smith in 1962 this way: "He just — I don't know. I was
leaving a restaurant where they wanted to raise the rent,
and I went up to Mr. Smith because I owed them some
money. I said, 'I'm leaving; I'm going in with Walter
Wencke to open a restaurant in the Electronics Building.'
He said, 'When are you going to have it?' I said, 'It won't
happen for eight or nine months.' He said, 'Do you want
to help me out [in the bank] that long?' I said, 'I never
done it [banking],' and he put me at a desk and didn't
introduce me [to the other employees]. He said, 'Stay
there.' So after the first month, I told him when I got my
check — and I never worked for no one there, I mean for
so many years I didn't know what it was — it was peanuts;
I, I told him I was quitting. He said, 'What?' I said, 'I'm
quitting.' He said, 'Do you know what you drew in this

month [in new business]?' He said, 'Over a half-million dollars.' He said, 'What the hell are you doing in the restaurant business? You belong here.' I said, 'Not for the money you're giving me.' He said, 'We're going to make you assistant vice-president and on the board of directors, too,' and he gave me a big thing — he gave me a paper, and I said, 'Where is the green stuff out here?' I said, 'I don't want any title unless I get paid for it.' I said, 'I'm too old for that.' He said, 'You're going to be here.' And they made me an assistant vice-president, and then in five months, vice-president — then baseball [vice-president of the Padres] just for the title, just for the tools to get it. . . .''

Lipton said he was given a straight salary with a new Continental every two years, and instead of cash bonuses for business brought in, he received shares of the bank's stock, which he sold to his brother, William Lipin, who already was one of the bank's largest stockholders.

William Lipin's career in San Diego was not harmed by his friendship with Frank DeSimone (they attended USC together — Lipin majoring in accounting and DeSimone in law; recognized as Mafia boss of Southern California until his death in 1967, DeSimone was one of two Californians arrested at Apalachin). One of Lipin's first accounts was the San Bernardo Winery in Escondido, then owned by Nick Lacata, who succeeded DeSimone as top Mafioso. Lipin's next client was the late Tony Mirabile, who ruled the San Diego Mafia for thirty years (after he was murdered in 1958, a check of his records revealed he had obtained loans totaling $850,000 from the U.S. National Bank). With Mirabile's help, Lipin and another brother, Bernard Lipinsky, branched out into the coin-operated machine business, and their B & B Enterprises had concessions at several military installations during World War II. (In April, 1969, C. Arnholt Smith announced that Westgate-California Corp. had sold the Kona Kai Club, including the Kona Inn and Voyager Restaurant, to William Lipin, his two brothers, Bernard Lipinsky and Lew Lipton, and his son-in-law, Don Cohn.)

In the meantime, Lew Lipton was making his mark in the city: in 1938, under the alias of Felix Aguilar, he was convicted of bookmaking (the record is missing from local police files). As a member of the draft board during World War II, he tried but failed to get an Army commission for DeSimone. (Recalling those days, one horse player said that Lipton's restaurant was a hangout for bettors and bookmakers. Every morning, around ten-thirty, Lipton would walk through and say, "Here come the judges for their coffee; clear out and come back in twenty minutes.") In 1956, when Fabio DeGregorio, a Sicilian in the United States on a visa (he was living with Salvatore Vitale, a notorious narcotics trafficker who mysteriously disappeared several years ago), visited Tijuana, Immigration decided it was a good place for him to stay. Lipton did not agree. He hired attorney Verne O. Warner to bring DeGregorio back into the bountiful home of Salvatore. When Immigration resisted Warner's appeal, DeGregorio married Vitale's daughter, Rose Marie, and

Rose Marie De Gregorio-
daughter of Rose & Frank Matran

applied for American citizenship. Immigration remained adamant. Lipton's next move was to have Warner write to Congressman Robert T. Wilson for a special bill, but when apprised of the Mafia and narcotics connections, Wilson declined.

(I am in possession of a copy of a birthday card, given to Tony Mirabile at a party in the Rainbow Gardens, which was inscribed by the local Mafia elite and their families — Frank Bompensiero; Maria, Clara, Vincent and Momo Adamo; Frances, Joe, Josephine, Vincent, Rose and Frank Matranga; Mr. and Mrs. Joe Ferraro; Mr. and Mrs. Charlie Pepitone; Onofrio Calamia; Joe and John [he signed it twice] LaMandri — and Lew and Aurora Lipton.)

At the time the Del Mar lease was under consideration, the executive committee of the nine-member board of the twenty-second Agriculture District was composed of a chairman, R. R. Richardson, and three members: Lipton, Harold McCormick and Harry Sugarman. Sugarman later resigned from the committee but remained a member of the board; he was succeeded by Robert O. Curran, the sole dissenter. Historically, the District Board has operated through a strong committee system, and with few exceptions committee recommendations are adopted in toto by the board.

The attorney general's report notes that "members of the Board openly held Mr. Alessio's business acumen in reverence, even feeling that he exhibited a 'Midas touch' in any transaction with which he dealt. This impression prevailed to the extent that it precluded the Board from endeavoring to secure documentation on Mr. Alessio's business operations, including the operation of racetracks. . . . The record on this question would be totally bare except for the steps independently taken by General Services to obtain information on the Caliente operation. . . . In contrast . . . is the Board's attitude toward the high bidder, the San Diego County Turf Club. The Executive Committee was openly dubious of their capabilities and formally requested specific data . . . an operational projection, and answers to a series of 17 questions to explain some of the assumptions in the projection. The responses . . . were treated . . . with incredulity, although . . . General Services and the Department of Agriculture . . . felt that the high bid was within the realm of feasibility."

C. Arnholt Smith wrote letters to legislators in support of Alessio's bid and telephoned McCormick at his home to personally voice his preference. When the board expressed a need for an accounting firm, Touche, Ross, Bailey and Smart, the regular auditor of Westgate-California, was retained. And when a need for an "expert" was felt, the board retained Robin Mansfield, executive vice-president and general manager for the Alessio Corporation, and secretary-treasurer of Del Mar Associates. Contrary to the Agricultural Code, which requires that all meetings of the board be open and public, the meetings were closed to the public.

The board received the percentage bids on September

12, 1966: San Diego County Turf Club, 18.21; Del Mar Associates, 11.42; Hollywood Turf Club, 10.25, and Del Mar Race Track, Inc., 8.26. The bids were referred to the executive committee for consideration. It was at this time that the San Diego County Turf Club was requested to produce its projection and other data. Nothing was sought from the other bidders. Michael Volpe, an employee of the district, nearly sabotaged the works when he reported that Del Mar Associates had underestimated its potential profit in the operation of the racetrack. It was this report and Mansfield's declaration that the high bid was not feasible to a successful operation, that brought about the employment of the auditor, Glen A. Olson, a partner in Touche, Ross, Bailey and Smart. When a meeting of the executive committee, to be held in Olson's office, did not materialize, Olson telephoned C. Arnholt Smith for instructions. According to the A.G.'s report, "Mr. Smith told Mr. Olson that he thought there were two projections that had been made that did not give the same results, leaving Mr. Olson with the impression that he was to reconcile the two projections. Mr. Smith also said that if it would be helpful in meeting the time deadline for Mr. Olson's work, delivery of the report to the District Board could be made through Mr. Smith's office." A few minutes later, Olson was summoned to Mansfield's office and given the two projections (the District's, which indicated net profits before rental to be 22.86 percent, and Mansfield's at 16.67 percent) and the figures of the San Diego County Turf Club. Olson quickly concluded that the comparison was not the duty of a C.P.A. and telephoned Smith to so advise him. Lipton and Roy Welch, a member of the board, contacted Olson, and persuaded him to compare the projected amounts with historical information and to make suggestions concerning areas requiring further analysis. The report was submitted the following day, but by then the board had already decided to award the lease to Del Mar Associates.

General Services was not entirely satisfied with the selection and requested an expansion of the executive committee's majority report. It was at this point that the board availed itself of Mansfield's expertise.

Six days later, on December 2, 1966, Olson was directed to attend a meeting in the board room of the U.S. National Bank. Gathered around a table when he arrived were Smith, Alessio, Mansfield, Lipton, Sugarman, McCormick and Ken Bojens, press agent for Caliente. Someone suggested that a report be prepared setting forth the method by which the board had reached its conclusions, and Olson was asked to assist in its authorship. He declined on "ethical" grounds. Three days later he was again called to a meeting, this time in Sugarman's offices, also located in the U.S. National Bank building, and it was then agreed that Olson's firm would type the final form of the committee's supplemental report, which was almost totally written by Mansfield.

The basic rationale expressed by the board in its refusal of the high bidder was that it would result in the failure of the operation to make a profit. On December 29, 1966,

General Services rejected the award to Del Mar Associates, and on February 18, 1967, the board again awarded the lease to Del Mar Associates, under a new plan calling for increased rentals of 15 percent for the first five years of the lease and 16.5 percent for the remaining fifteen years, an average of 16.11 percent, plus an agreement to underwrite $12 million for capital improvement and to raise the annual rental guarantee to $1.2 million.

"There appears to be no documentary evidence submitted to the Executive Committee by Del Mar Associates or in fact relied upon by the Board members which would show that the new bid percentages of Del Mar Associates would permit a profitable operation," the attorney general's report concluded. "In fact, the operational projection submitted by Del Mar Associates to [General Services] indicated an extremely small margin of profit at the 11.2 percent figure. This concern for profits was the alleged basic rejection to awarding the bid to the high bidder. . . . there clearly was no equality of treatment of the bidders by the Board. In this regard, the retention of . . . Mansfield . . . as an expert adviser raises serious ethical and legal questions. The entire procedure endangers the sanctity of the sealed bid in California public bidding situations."

Alessio: "Since that day there has been harassment of my brother Russ, a war veteran, an honor war veteran. They are trying to harass me now. I don't know why. If there's any laws I've violated; I think if there's anything wrong, can't they call an individual down and say to them, 'Well, you did this wrong.' Is there anything wrong in life, 'cause I've been here thirty-eight years, and I have the confidence of these people. I have run their businesses for them, there is nothing wrong with that. Every time I turn around, one of these Mexicans want me to be their interpreter; there's nothing wrong with that. Right today I had two of the Mexican treasury men that I acted as interpreter for them. And they speak of very confidential situations. During the Second World War, I played a big part, because I spoke Italian and Spanish. It just doesn't make sense."

In the spring and summer of 1967, Russell Alessio, manager of Caliente's Foreign Book, and sixteen others were arrested on suspicion of bookmaking by Internal Revenue Service agents, who described Alessio as the kingpin of the operation. The presence of a bookmaking ring in its city did not stir too much excitement in San Diego's Copley press, which devoted barely an inch to Alessio's arrest — on the obituary page. Without television, few would have learned of this "harassment." Among the bookmaking locations identified in the charges were Russell's palatial home in El Cajón and the Palomar Inn (midpoint between San Diego and Tijuana), which is operated by Tony and Frank Balistrieri, sons of Francesco "Big Frank" Balistrieri, a Sicilian immigrant who was powerful in Milwaukee Democratic circles before moving on to San Diego. His nephew, Frank Peter Balistrieri, was recently named by the FBI as the Mafia's top man in Milwaukee. The seventeen suspects

were indicted on multiple counts of failing to purchase
fifty-dollar occupational tax stamps for wagering (since
ruled unconstitutional by the Supreme Court); Alessio
was also charged with "interstate and foreign transmission
of wagering information and foreign travel in aid of rack-
eteering enterprises."

A customs agent describes what happened when IRS
agents arrived at the port at San Ysidro to arrest Russell.
"As I understand it, they first went to his residence at
seven in the morning but he had already left for the track.
Well, they put his license-plate number on the line, and
you should have seen the reaction of the inspectors. To a
man (there were about eight on duty) they rushed to the
agents and said, 'You made a mistake. This is one of Mr.
Alessio's cars.' They know the license number of every
Alessio car that crosses the border. Well, they were fit to
be tied. First thing you know, the IRS boys are apologiz-
ing, saying things like, 'I didn't issue the arrest warrant,
the commissioner did. Don't blame me, I'm just doing my
job.' And all the time, the inspectors are looking at them
like, as if to say, 'Don't you understand? This is the
brother of Mr. Alessio you're talking about; the wonderful
man who gives us a free dinner on Sunday.' For years,
John has been sending Sunday dinner to the boys on the
line. It's cheap *mordida* on John's part, but to these guys,
it's really a gift from God. When Russ finally came across,
the only things he carried in his car or on his person were
an honorary deputy sheriff's badge, an honorary highway
patrolman's plate, rosary beads, a Saint Christopher

medal and a picture of his daughter, which showed, I suppose, that he's religious, a good family man and certainly important within the community." Russell Alessio was convicted and received a three-year suspended prison sentence and was fined $10,000 — this was his second conviction, the first being in 1943, at which time he paid a small fine.

Alessio: "Oh yeah, oh yeah. Some people have been critical. You can see what's happening today. We testified in Sacramento. We showed them we bid properly." They point to a conflict of interest. "That's right. But what could be the conflict of interest when, I, an American citizen, our entities that we have in San Diego, what would be the conflict of interest?" The attorney general referred to Lipton . . . "Well, naturally, our enemies are going to use that and more, but the bidding says that whoever bids for this racetrack has to be a bona fide businessman. They have to qualify; they don't necessarily have to be the best bidder. I'm sure that in the group we had there, there is not one you can say isn't a reputable businessman. They are all very successful businessmen in the state of California, especially in the San Diego area. But they used that, very much so. So the whole thing is, everything is status quo." He pauses and looks about him, at all the great men hanging on the walls, at the photographs of the eleven schools, and on to the window, oblivious to the rain rattling down in a blinding deluge. His dark eyes, hugely magnified behind the thick lenses, are troubled as they come to rest on the tape recorder.

"Turn that thing off. I'd like to talk to you personally. I want to level with you. I'm going to tell you the real story, but it's going to be off the record. I don't want you writing about it." When the offer is declined, he slowly leans back in the big chair, his hands folding piously across his chest, his square jaw, a jutting banner of strength, suddenly fragile with age. "Unfortunately, people misinterpret these things," he says, his head caught in a spasm of incomprehensibility. "God has been good with me and had me down here for thirty-eight years. I've worked very, very hard, and, so to say, promoted these ideas, but some people misrepresent these ideas. It is very, very unfortunate that this world is getting so vicious in that type of attitude." Misrepresent motives? "They misrepresent why it is that Mr. Alessio is so well liked. They don't go back and say he's been down there for thirty-eight years. I came here as a young man, that was my destiny, the way God wanted it, and I've been very, very happy."

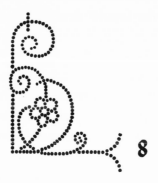

8

La Reforma
Última

It is possible for an American to enter Canada at Niagara
Falls and exit at Detroit and not be aware that he was in a
foreign country. This is inconceivable on the Mexican
border. Mexico, as writer Carlos Fuentes observed, is the
nearest reminder the United States has of the realities of
life outside the affluent society, "a practical, everyday
reminder that life does not everywhere conform to the
American plan."

But does life on the border conform to the Mexican
plan? Is the border really Mexico? And the answer, as far
as I was able to determine, is a resounding Yes! The principal difference is façade. Mexico City is the Great Façade. Of the eight million people, one-sixth of the entire

population, squeezed within its boundaries, how many thousands stand before the façade? And how many millions struggle hopelessly behind it, in what *capitolinos* call the *cinto de misterio* — the belt of mystery — but more accurately, the belt of poverty.

All large bordertowns have their belts of mystery known as *periferias,* periphery, and inhabited by *paracaidistas,* parachutists — this term compliments their stealth in descending on a town in the night and encircling it with a ring of mud *colonias* by morning. The emphasis on speed makes it all the more inevitable.

It is the *paracaidista,* the landless peasant in quest of gringo dollars, who has ballooned the populace of bordertowns tenfold in two decades: approximately 500,000 live in Juárez, 400,000 in Mexicali, 300,000 in Tijuana, 130,-000 in Matamoros, and 60,000, more or less, in Nuevo Laredo, Reynosa, Piedras Negras, Acuña and Nogales. How accurate are these figures? "We have two methods of taking the census, *señor.* One is to walk into a *colonia* and throw a peso in the street. The other is to count each window and multiply by twelve."

Swollen figures have not changed the character of the bordertown. It remains a town, not a city, without governmental powers (reposed in state and federal aeries) or civic responsibility (not even a library in Tijuana). Streets and services like sewage, water, gas, and electricity are either nonexistent or in states of perpetual chaos.

Bordertowns defy societal categorization. They exist on the osmosis of tourism: thirty-six million annual border crossings in Juárez, twenty-four million in Tijuana, and tens of millions everywhere else — these figures represent all crossings through American gates, by tourists as well as Mexicans. The *paracaidista*, if he cannot emigrate *al otro lado*, must try somehow to scrounge a living from the careless droppings of celebrating gringos. This is tedious and demeaning, and not conducive to the good amigo policy.

Drive into any bordertown (except Tijuana) and there will be a walking parking meter awaiting you when you stop. He will open the door for you, smile his greeting, and assure you that all will be well until your return. (If you reject him, all will not be so well.) Drive in at nine in the evening and return at five in the morning and he will be there, waiting and smiling, and offering you an opportunity to make his day for him. Most walking parking meters will cover one side of a block, feeding five-centavo coins into meters only when policemen appear. Police in most bordertowns remove the license plates of cars illegally parked.

Drive past the neon lights and through the slums and find, if you can, suburbia. There you will see another Mexican tradition that dates back to the Spanish viceroys — the *velador*. He is the fellow who sits before a house all night to make sure that other fellows in his economic straits do not burglarize it. Anybody who owns anything has a *velador* to protect it. Hot or cold, rain or dry or snow, he sits and watches, a whistle dangling from his neck his only weapon.

In Piedras Negras, I discovered that the American consul, Howard Walker, did not have a *velador*. How come? "Well, no one has ever come around and said, 'Look, I'm your *velador*.' So I presume I don't need one. You have to pay them, of course, but people get them because there's not too much police protection — the city can't afford it. We do have an Army garrison with one general and fifteen men, but a very nice general."

A slum is a slum is a slum — but not really. Here in Mexico it is an institutional phenomenon that started with the Spanish conquest of 1519, and has since revolutionized man's concept of slums. In Mexico City, each generation is entitled to build its own slums in the ruins of its predecessors. This allows for the innovation of the latest building materials used in packing crates. In the bordertowns, they start from scratch; however, in Tijuana I did see a new shack perched precariously atop an old one. Here a man's abode will depend on how clever a scavenger or bold a thief he proves himself to be in an enterprise that is highly competitive.

Urbanization in Mexico is proceeding at a faster clip than almost anywhere else in the world, and the reason for this is the failure of the land-reform program and the migration off the land of a displaced peasantry. Land is more expensive here than in the United States. Savings go into land instead of into stocks and banks — real status is to own a ranch. The other edge to this problem is that industry, particularly on the border, is equally primitive in its development.

There is a culture of poverty in Mexico, religious in its fatalism, that teaches that nothing can be done about one's lot in life: "Don't oppose the will of God," or "He who was born to be a pot doesn't leave the kitchen." It is perhaps this philosophy, more than anything else, that has kept Mexico from being ignited by the contagion of political violence that has swept far more affluent nations. But the government is darkly apprehensive, finding "Communist plots" behind every protest. Recently, when a small band of peasants, presumably leftists, clumsily attacked an army garrison in Madera, they were pursued into the hills, killed and dragged back to be strung up in the plaza as an example to other incipient insurrectionists. When students in Mexico City staged a protest demonstration in September, 1968, police opened fire with machine guns, killing fifteen and wounding many others, including journalists and innocent bystanders. This harsh overreacting is typical in revolution-oriented Latin republics. Any form of protest terrifies the Establishment.

But television, which somehow finds its way into many humble hovels, may do for Mexico what the Revolution promised but failed to achieve — convince the people that there is a better life and that the will of God is open to collective bargaining.

"I used to get upset about the shacks in Tijuana," a woman reporter told me, "until friends of mine who have traveled extensively in Mexico pointed out that to the people in the interior, these are their well-to-do cousins up here." Everything is relative, *sí, señor?*

When a group of service clubs in San Diego and other Southwest communities attempted to send truckloads of food and building supplies to the Indians of San Felipe following a disastrous flood, the proudful rich in Mexico City refused their aid.

Thousands of Indians have found their way to the border. "It is a bad situation," a wealthy Mexican merchant explained. "You never see a man with his woman, but you see the woman, pregnant, holding a child and dragging another. And these hardy, these poor, sweet, little Indian boys, all they can do is stick out their hand. And the woman, she doesn't know what it is not to be pregnant. Birth control pills? They don't know what an aspirin is, let alone birth control pills. In the United States, a girl goes out: 'Hey, honey, you forgot your pill.' 'Oh, Mother, thank you!' The old man, he comes to the bridge, drinking *mezcal* and maybe he'll try to hustle a couple pesos. There was a time in Tijuana when you never saw a cat. Now you see a few. The story was the Indians did something with them. It's possible if you're hungry enough, yes? A big problem is that most Indians don't speak Spanish. They live like gypsies, the women beg and the men drink and fuck."

Of the seven hundred tribal groups that existed at the time of the Conquest, some fifty have survived the physical mutilations and economic deprivations of the past four centuries. Most Mexicans I talked with appeared genuinely sympathetic to the plight of the Indian; but, in point of fact, the Indian is the most shunted, the most despised creature in Mexico. No mestizo will admit to Indian blood, and if the slant of eyes or angle of nose is in the least suggestive, the moustache is there to dispute it. No self-respecting Mexican will be without wheat bread in his home — it is the one food that separates him from the tortilla-eating Indian. The only good Indian is a rich Indian — once an Indian gains wealth, he ceases culturally to be an Indian.

Yet Indianism is ubiquitous in Mexican culture. Its influence is found everywhere — in architecture, music, religion, all art forms. Even modern skyscrapers reflect the brilliant hues of the Indian palette. The Mexican's manic-depressive tendency (one moment gallant-effusive-warm-happy; the next, withdrawn, lost in inexplicable grief) is an Indian characteristic.

The *mañana* syndrome is an Indian hangup. Indian time was a happening of no yesterday, today or tomorrow — a circle without numbers. A group of successful Mexicans can make lunch head-reelingly pleasant. It may begin at noon; and by the time you are ready to stagger out, unfed, at four, there are still a half-dozen fresh drinks stacked up before you. The tempo is set by the fastest drinker, and nobody flashes money; somehow it is taken care of. Ashamedly, you are the only one to bring up the existence of time. The others are warmly immersed in nostalgic reminiscence of first confrontation with man's most implacable quarry — poosy. "The first time was with my aunt when I was twelve. I was baby-sitting and she came in late and found me in her bed" — shades of

Boccaccio. The second most fascinating subject is money; not one's own personal fortune, but what everybody else has paid for their possessions. The degree of interest is on a sliding scale of inflation. A house is *really* a house when it has cost a million pesos or more. Business is confined to the office and never intrudes on more important subjects. Wives are never mentioned. The Mexican's pathological fear of being cuckolded is legendary, and court annals record the flights of violence that have issued from his vivid imagination.

The institution of the *casa chica* (the little house for the mistress — sometimes the *chica* is bigger than the wife's *grande*) continues. I know of one wealthy Mexican in Monterrey who has eleven mistresses and forty-six children, and all the older ones drive new Fords. In his social class, this is the ultimate in *machismo*, the cult of masculinity so important to Mexicans. To be *muy macho* means to be very manly in a rawly sensitive context. A good bullfighter is *macho*; a poor Indian who defends an insult (real or imaginary) with a knife is *macho*; the mestizo, like the rich hidalgo he emulates, prefers a gun. Death is a small sacrifice, indeed, when one's honor is in the balance.

In two seasons of following the *corrida de toros*, Nancy, the attractive blonde who followed bullfighters, met many rich Mexicans with a yen for blond, statuesque gringas. "They are so gallant," she says. "Nothing is too good for you when you're out with them. Flowers, candy, champagne, expensive trinkets. There's no one in the world

richer than a rich Mexican. They are fantastically extravagant. And the words. Oh, on and on. They bring music,
they whip you around the dance floor, they stare into your
eyes. At first it makes you feel like you are the only person
on earth. But it's phony — they are sincerely doing it in-
sincerely. After a while, you feel like saying, 'Cool it,
remember me; I've been here before, so let's be friends
and have a good conversation.' On the streets anywhere in
Mexico, you can't walk a block without a dozen cars
honking at you. One time in Guadalajara a Mexican
actually drove up a tree. It was so embarrassing. And on
the sidewalk, they're always whispering things in your
ear — you're beautiful, you're lovely — very nice compliments but so much of it is tied up with *macho*, like they
want their friends to see them doing it. It's unusual for a
lone Mexican to do more than smile or nod when he's on
foot.

"The thing that really excites Mexicans are personal
references. They are so wrapped up in their honor, it's
amazing. And you never hear the word *madre*, not even
when you're saying something like 'It's your mother on
the phone.' Even then it's '*tu mamá*.' It's the same with
their wives, you can't mention them. It's a thing they
have about women and mothers. The most horrendous
insult is five taps of the horn, like shave-and-a-hair-cut; it
spells out *Chinga su madre*" (literally, motherfucker).
"You can make it even worse by adding two more taps,
cabrón, which means cuckold. I've seen a boy pulled
bodily out the window of his car because his girlfriend
innocently tapped the horn five times in front of a friend's

house. This man came out of nowhere, and first thing we knew the boy was lying in the street unconscious. But the word *chinga* is found everywhere in Mexico, part of the restroom graffiti. And you hear it on the street all the time; women use it constantly, but it doesn't have much meaning until it's coupled with *madre*.

"The Mexicans I knew spent hours grooming. Two and three shoeshines a day, constantly being manicured, facials, steambaths, fussy little barbering details, and just drenched in perfume. They don't spend too much time working. Boy, do they protect themselves. I would ask somebody if he knew whether so-and-so was married, and invariably the answer would be, 'Oh, I've never seen him with a wife.' And do they love to be seen with a pretty American girl. I think they love it more than sex itself. It's more *macho*."

From my hotel window in El Paso, I watched the snow drift softly toward the brown mudhuts on the brown hills of the brown *paracaidistas* — a sepia print of a mock bombed-out Jerusalem. Soon everything would be antiseptically white, and hundreds would die because of it.

Perched on the hills above Juárez, gathered like armies of refugees in exodus, gypsies in the un-Promised Land, without roads, electricity, gas, sewers, or water, they are privileged spectators to the scenic wonders of good roads, neon lights, glittering automobiles, palatial homes and kidney-shaped swimming pools. It is inspiring to look down. Few people look up.

Guidebook writers are fond of Latins who have a "peculiar talent for gaiety" in the midst of squalor. Strange, I found so little gaiety. Yet I think I gave it a fair test. I found enough squalor to satisfy the greediest wallower.

Periodically, U.S. magazines and newspapers herald the millennium to end all millenniums, reform to end all reforms, cleanup to end all cleanups, but the more things are predicted to change, the easier it is for the predictors to propagate the status quo.

After arresting a hundred prostitutes in 1947, the Inspector General announced: "This is just another move to set a higher moral standard for the City of Tijuana. We will continue to follow this procedure until the town is the cleanest in all Mexico."

In 1961, Antonio "Tony" Bermúdez promised to transform the whole sixteen-hundred-mile border into "The Longest Show Window in the World." Bermúdez, who made his first fortune as a wholesale liquor distributor in Prohibition days, was mayor of Juárez in the Forties, head of PEMEX (the nationalized oil industry) for ten years, a federal senator, an ambassador-at-large in the Middle East, and most recently — at the time of his 1961 announcement — director of PRONAF — Programa Nacional de Reforma Frontezia — the border rehabilitation program.

His program, as reported in Newsweek, August 7, 1961, "is a costly one, but Bermúdez expects it eventually to pay for itself. As a starter this week, bulldozers will begin moving earth in the 550-acre river bottom land in the center of Tijuana. . . . A $15 million flood control and reclamation project will be topped by landscaped boulevards, new parks, and new administration buildings. In the process, the rest of the city, which has long been notorious for its tourist clip joints, prostitutes, and marijuana peddlers, will be cleaned up, or cleaned out." That marijuana smoke is potent stuff.

Seven years later, Mayor López had this to say about the flood control–reclamation project. "At the beginning we were interested in building the channel and the U.S. wasn't, you see. So after we made our plans, the U.S. accepted to do their part. So we had to change our whole plan again. We have commission between Mexico and the U.S., the Water Limit Commission, I think it's named, and we have stipulation where we discuss these things. But if we approve something, it's got to go to Washington and Sacramento, and also to Mexicali and Mexico City. By the time it comes back, something new comes out and we have to discuss it again. And so the whole thing keeps going around in circles, you see. It will take some time now before we get together on it. But it will be very beautiful when finished. It will be the future of Tijuana."

". . . There will be other projects going on simultaneously in all border areas," *Newsweek* continued. "One town, Reinosa [*sic* Reynosa] . . . is considered so hopeless that a new bridge will be built so tourists can bypass it. . . . Hopeful of attracting more respectable U.S. dollars across the border, Bermúdez has called for new comfort facilities, new public services, and new hotels, motels, and shopping centers for visitors."

This — on a minutely limited scale — has been precisely PRONAF's contribution: Palm Springs–type motels
and shopping centers for gringos which do nothing more
for the community than accent its squalor.

The latest word on cleanups came from the New York
Times on November 12, 1967: "For the last two years
City Hall [Tijuana] has been occupied by a young team
headed by 39-year-old Mayor Francisco López Gutiérrez,
who has been trying to change Tijuana's reputation. . . .
Observers here agree that the new administration is
more interested in improving the city than in lining its
pockets, and is willing to stand up to those with extensive
financial interests in maintaining vice. With cooperation
from the state and federal governments, municipal services have been vastly improved, the streets and border
entry have been made more attractive, and an effort has
begun to 'clean up' Revolution Avenue, the main tourist
street."

"It is very difficult," Mayor López told me, "because,
you see, I don't have any jurisdiction inside a house — a
place of business, you know, or a home, too. Unless somebody is killing somebody and calls for help, then we can
go in. But to investigate if a crime is being committed,
that is the job of the state and federal police. What I do,
you see, is tell the governor about certain things and
sometimes he orders it done. So the cleanup is by the
governor, not me. I'm only the stool pigeon."

As the mayor talked, *El Presidente* gazed down upon us
from his perch of honor on the wall, a faint benevolent

smile in his dark eyes. And what a splendid image he radiated to all the people — *El Presidente*, seated in a gold chair, under a gold eagle, in a gold frame, within a gold frame, within a gold frame.

And I thought of all the splendid reforms awaiting the *muchachos* of the *paracaidistas — la reforma última*. And then I was reminded of a story told by a San Diego reporter of a recent national press junket to Tijuana, and how it ended up in San Diego's Mission Valley with American whores. And how impressed they were with the mayor, him being so young and handsome and liberal, and what a truly "nice guy" he was for promising so many splendid reforms.

Index

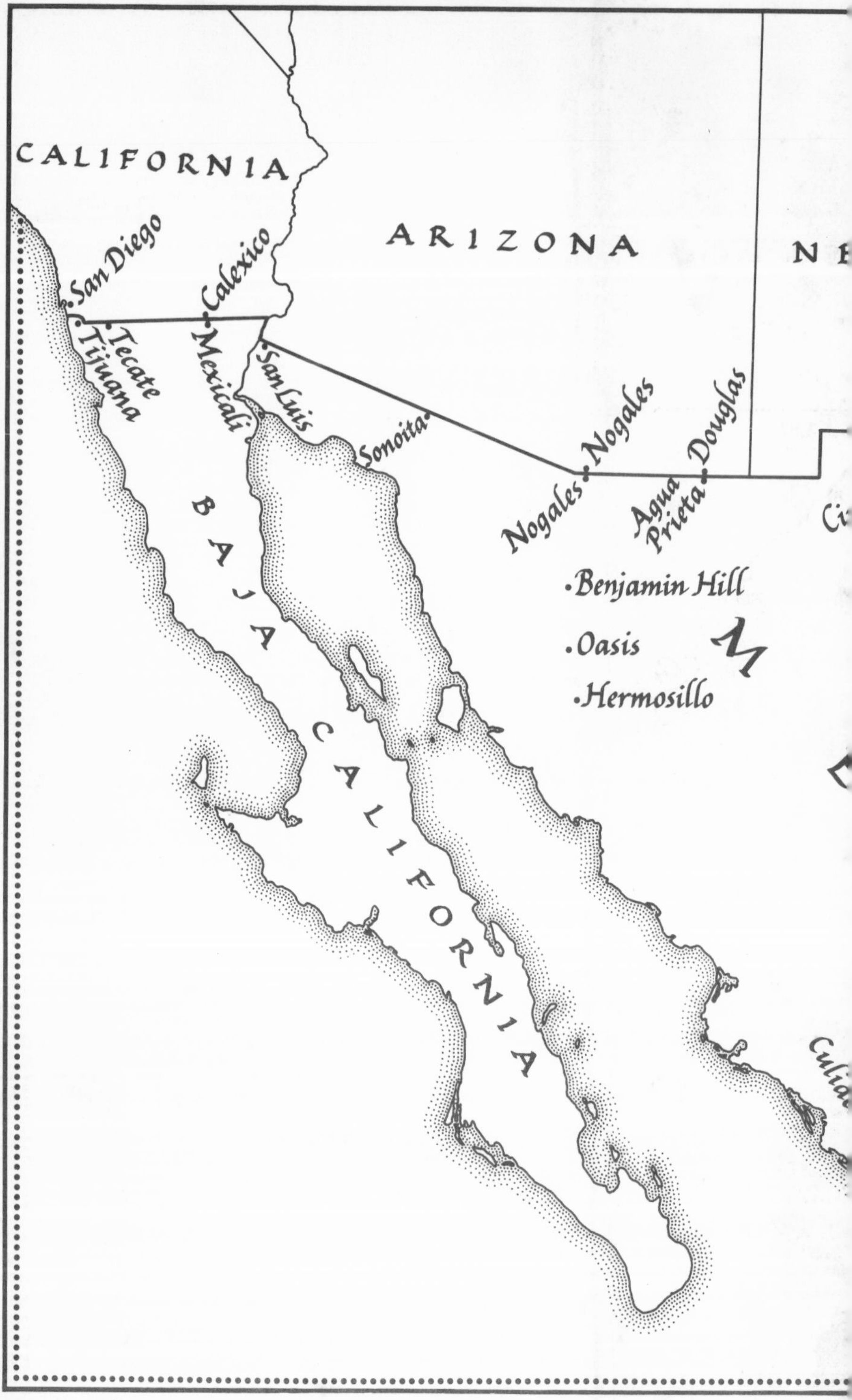
CALIFORNIA
ARIZONA
San Diego
Calexico
Tecate
Tijuana
Mexicali
San Luis
Sonoita
Nogales
Nogales
Douglas
Agua Prieta
Benjamin Hill
Oasis
Hermosillo
BAJA CALIFORNIA